Whistling in the Dark

In Pursuit of the Nightingale

RICHARD MABEY

Whistling in the Dark

In Pursuit of the Nightingale

SINCLAIR-STEVENSON

First published in Great Britain in 1993
by Sinclair-Stevenson
an imprint of Reed Consumer Books Ltd
Michelin House, 81 Fulham Road, London sw3 6rb
and Auckland, Melbourne, Singapore and Toronto

A CIP catalogue record for this book
is available at the British Library

ISBN 1 85619 176 1

Phototypeset by Intype, London
Printed and bound in Great Britain
by Clays Ltd, St Ives plc

Contents

The scraperboard illustrations
are by
Peter Viccars

Prologue

This book does not set out to be an ornithological study of the nightingale, nor a history of literary responses to its song. If anything it is about the bird's remarkable capacity to undermine such neat ways of parcelling up experiences. In *The Charm of Birds*, Grey of Fallodon wrote that 'the nightingale's song has compass, variety and astonishing power; it arrests attention and compels admiration; it has onset and impact; but it is fitful, broken and restless: it is a song to listen to, but not live with.' It can also be unsettlingly evocative. Poets muse about its biological meaning, and hard-bitten zoologists are drawn into meditations on its musicality and the possibility that it might be evidence of something like real creativity.

But there are no clear answers. In its cultural history as in its real life the nightingale remains an elusive, mercurial bird. It is migratory, nocturnal, suggestive. Even when it is heard (or celebrated) in full-throated performance, there is always the sense of something beyond or behind the song. It must be stalked, as John Clare did (p. 85), hunting 'like a very boy/Creeping on hands & knees through matted thorns/[to where] All seemed as hidden as a thought unborn.'

Whistling in the Dark is an episodic account of such a pursuit, through the matted thickets of medieval poetry, adolescent romanticism and animal psychology, and the scrubby wastes where they overlap.

Richard Mabey
1993

For L.G., with love

from
The Flower and the Leaf

On Philomel I fixed my whole desire,
And listened for the queen of all the choir;
Fain would I hear her heavenly voice to sing,
And wanted yet an omen of the spring . . .

   . . . When she I sought, the nightingale, replied:
So sweet, so shrill, so variously she sung,
That the grove echoed, and the valleys rung;
And I so ravished with her heavenly note,
I stood entranced, and had no room for thought,
But all o'erpowered with ecstasy of bliss,
Was in a pleasing dream of paradise;
At length I waked, and looking round the bower,
Searched every tree, and pried on every flower,
If anywhere by chance I might espy
The rural poet of the melody;
For still methought she sung not far away:
At last I found her on a laurel spray.
Close by my side she sat, and fair in sight,
Full in a line against her opposite;
Where stood with eglantine the laurel twined,
And both their native sweets were well conjoined.
  On the green bank I sat, and listened long;
(Sitting was more convenient for the song:)
Nor till her lay was ended could I move,
But wished to dwell for ever in the grove.
Only methought the time too swiftly passed,
And every note I feared would be the last.
My sight, and smell, and hearing, were employed,
And all three senses in full gust enjoyed.
And what alone did all the rest surpass,
The sweet possession of the fairy place;

Single, and conscious to myself alone
Of pleasures to the excluded world unknown;
Pleasures which nowhere else were to be found,
And all Elysium in a spot of ground.

Anon, late 15th century
Adapted by John Dryden, 1700

1

'All Elysium in a spot of ground'

It is early May, a nightingale moon. I'm perched in a
narrow lane above the Stour valley in Suffolk, listening to
the birds. The landscape is already drained of colour,
caught in that moment between light and dark when distances and outlines blur. I try to focus on the tumulus of
scrub in front of me, but it seems to be dancing and
flashing with phosphorescence. I know this is just my
eyes playing tricks, but it gives the undergrowth an oddly
insubstantial feel, quite out of keeping with the brilliant
clarity of the song that is pouring from it.

It is my first nightingale of the year, and a coloratura
bird into the bargain. It has a clipped, Latin style, full of
deft phrases which are turned this way and that and
teased out into short, fading tremolos. As the moon rises,
changing from hazy orange to platinum white, the singing
becomes more assured. The sound is astonishingly pure
and penetrating, broken with teasing, theatrical silences.
I realise I am rooted to the spot, standing in the middle
of the lane and barely noticing the cars edging past.

No other bird song can match these outpourings under the May full moon. Even by nightingale standards they seem more eloquent and passionate than at any other time of the spring. Perhaps this is just a flight of fancy on my part, a touch of moonshine. But it is a critical moment in the birds' year. Ever since early April nightingales have been migrating back to Europe from their wintering quarters in tropical Africa, running the gauntlet of bird-catchers and Mediterranean storms. The advance guard are almost all male birds, and since their arrival they will have been scouting out nesting territories in woodland thickets and river valleys. The females follow a week or so later, choosing warm, clear nights for migration if possible. These nights in early May mark the crescendo of the nightingales' courtship. Territories are settled, female birds are on the move and choosing mates, and the last waves of new arrivals are winging in. No wonder the males' songs seem so intense: they are serenades to tempt the females down from the sky.

Did Tennyson know about this when he wrote of how 'the music of the moon/Sleeps in the plain eggs of the nightingale'? The birds have always excited wild imaginings, and they have often lured me into wildly unexpected situations. This spring of all springs, I hadn't expected to be listening to them in the austere landscape of East Anglia. It was meant to be Portugal, with the woman in whose company I had trailed nightingales across northern Europe all the previous spring. Lily and I had planned to share our first birds of the year under the almond blossom in Alentejo. But the relationship faltered (plenty of singing but no shared territory) and we went our separate ways.

The spring after we parted was, as any good romantic is entitled to expect, dismal and pinching. Snow fell at Easter. The summer migrants were a whole month late. When the swifts finally arrived in early May – a thin, defiant arrow of birds careering in from the east as I was coming home from the shops – I was so relieved to see

4

them that I drove the car into the kerb. But they proved
to be the best of omens, and within two days England
was suffused by exquisite, balmy weather. Having no
stomach for moping alone by the Mediterranean, I sped
to East Anglia, where I had first been bewitched by nightingales twenty years before.

Standing in this clamorous Suffolk lane, I don't feel it
is that bad a swap. The moon is high enough to cast
shadows now, and this virtuoso in front of me is unreeling
my memories . . . South-west France, the previous June.
The last nightingales of the year, up in a mist in the
Corbières hills with Lily. Our very first nightingale
together in the Dordogne, and the walnut liqueur we gig-
gled our way through that evening in celebration. The
year before that, and a miserable late April in the Provençal hilltop village of Les Baux. The mistral had blown for
almost the whole week I was there, freezing out any hint
of spring. Then, on the final day, I had woken to a brilliant
sky and the sight of packs of alpine swifts hurtling round
the medieval walls – and, down in the valley, the sound
of a nightingale and hoopoe calling in concert.

The nightingale's song can do this, seeming frothy and
funny one minute, then setting mundane puzzles – how
does it utter some of those notes through a closed bill? –
before plunging you again into resonant thickets of
memory . . . This time of bad weather, and of brave
stands made by the birds. Three singing into the teeth of
an April gale from bushy shell-craters on the Tyneham
military ranges in Dorset. A brave scattering on the last
remnants of John Clare's Emmonsales Heath, in a gloomy
May fog. An absurd, fleeting pang for a favourite cotton
jumper I used to wear on cold evening vigils. Some lost
struggles, too. Thirty-four nightingales found dead on a
beach at Cadiz after a violent thunderstorm in April '91.
And back home again that summer, empty woods, silent
heaths and the realisation that the bird is vanishing across

5

much of its traditional range in central and southern England.

There is a lull in the singing, a huge, emphatic silence that seems to be part of the performance. It is about ten o'clock and the moon is almost at its height. By Suffolk standards I am on the top of the world. Below me, Arger Fen arches like a whaleback across the whole span of the southern horizon. Everywhere, dead elm stumps rear in silhouette amongst the scrub. The light is extraordinary – luminous, dusty, giving every pale surface the lustre of mother-of-pearl. Mounds of cow parsley and scythed grass glow in the moonbeams like suspended balls of mist. By the side of the lane I catch the scents of broom and bluebells, a blend of coconut and honey, the exotic and the homely, that has something of the ripened quality of the song itself.

I have wandered down the lane to a stream at the edge of the fen wood. There are bats hawking round the alders – silent, flickering shadows against the twigs. I wonder if their exquisitely high-tuned ears pick up nightingales. What can a nightingale sound like to a bat? For that matter, what does a bat sound like to a nightingale?

At about 10.30, the silence is broken. The bird on the ridge has started up again, in the same patch of scrub as before. It is a quarter of a mile away, and this far off its song is almost percussive, like the sound of greenwood spitting in a fire. I begin to pick up other noises in the distance as I hurry back along the lane. A peacock, dogs, a tawny owl and a desultory, inferior nightingale somewhere to the north, soon shamed into silence by this remarkable singer.

He is louder and more extravagant now, and seems to be rehearsing the whole nightingale repertoire. He sings a stylish four-note phrase, then repeats it in a minor key. He slides into a bubbling tremolo on a single note and holds it for more than ten seconds. How does he breathe?

I cannot believe he is not consciously improvising. I want to clap – and with barely credible timing, a shooting star arcs over the bush in which he is singing.

I am edging closer without realising it and am now no more than ten feet away. Nothing stops the flow of notes. They fill the air, they seem to be solid, to be doing odd things to the light. I am half-aware that my peripheral vision is closing down, and that I am riveted to the bush by this tunnel of intense sound.

I remember Keats's enrapturement, and Shelley's lines 'Sounds overflow the listener's brain/So sweet, that joy is almost pain'. I draw back a little. But I can't sense any melancholy or anguish in my own response, only a slight sadness that I am listening to this stupendous performer on my own.

But the effort breaks the spell and I start to walk back to the car. The bird begins to recede, 'Past the near meadows, over the still stream,/Up the hill-side; and now 'tis buried deep . . .', and I am left, puzzling again over how another species, supposedly going about the routine business of defining its territory, can have such an extraordinary effect on one's senses and emotions.

from
Ode to a Nightingale

My heart aches, and a drowsy numbness pains
 My sense, as though of hemlock I had drunk,
Or emptied some dull opiate to the drains
 One minute past, and Lethe-wards had sunk:
'Tis not through envy of thy happy lot,
 But being too happy in thy happiness, —
  That thou, light-winged Dryad of the trees,
   In some melodious plot
 Of beechen green, and shadows numberless,
  Singest of summer in full-throated ease.

O, for a draught of vintage! that hath been
 Cool'd a long age in the deep-delved earth,
Tasting of Flora and the country green,
 Dance, and Provençal song, and sunburnt mirth!
O for a beaker full of the warm South,
 Full of the true, the blushful Hippocrene,
  With beaded bubbles winking at the brim,
   And purple-stained mouth;
 That I might drink, and leave the world unseen,
  And with thee fade away into the forest dim:

Fade far away, dissolve, and quite forget
 What thou amongst the leaves hast never known,
The weariness, the fever, and the fret
 Here, where men sit and hear each other groan;
Where palsy shakes a few, sad, last gray hairs,
 Where youth grows pale, and spectre-thin, and dies;
  Where but to think is to be full of sorrow
   And leaden-eyed despairs,
 Where Beauty cannot keep her lustrous eyes,
  Or new Love pine at them beyond to-morrow . . .

Darkling I listen; and, for many a time
　　I have been half in love with easeful Death,
Call'd him soft names in many a mused rhyme,
　　To take into the air my quiet breath;
Now more than ever seems it rich to die,
　　To cease upon the midnight with no pain,
　　　　While thou art pouring forth thy soul abroad
　　　　　In such an ecstasy!
　　　Still wouldst thou sing, and I have ears in vain —
　　　　To thy high requiem become a sod.

Thou wast not born for death, immortal Bird!
　　No hungry generations tread thee down;
The voice I hear this passing night was heard
　　In ancient days by emperor and clown:
Perhaps the self-same song that found a path
　　Through the sad heart of Ruth, when, sick for home,
　　　She stood in tears amid the alien corn;
　　　　The same that oft-times hath
　　Charm'd magic casements, opening on the foam
　　　Of perilous seas, in faery lands forlorn.

Forlorn! the very word is like a bell
　　To toll me back from thee to my sole self!
Adieu! the fancy cannot cheat so well
　　As she is fam'd to do, deceiving elf.
Adieu! adieu! thy plaintive anthem fades
　　Past the near meadows, over the still stream,
　　　Up the hill-side; and now 'tis buried deep
　　　　In the next valley-glades:
　　Was it a vision, or a waking dream?
　　　Fled is that music: – Do I wake or sleep?

John Keats, 1819

2

'Immortal Bird'

When Keats called the nightingale the 'immortal Bird', he was talking of the way the bird's song seemed to transcend the individual, mortal singer, and how it had been an immemorial antidote to decay and grief. But he could well have been remarking on its extraordinary persistence as a symbol in Western culture. It is hard to think of another wild creature which has had such a versatile and honoured role. At various times the nightingale has served as a kind of parish familiar or local wood-spirit; as a symbol, and messenger, of love; as a harbinger of spring and an arche-type of natural music. Aristophanes called it 'peerless in song'. In 630 AD, the monk Aldhelm of Malmesbury made it the subject of a riddle, that played on the irony of a small brown bird acquiring such a musical reputation: 'Mean is my colour but none hath scorned my song.'

It has long been the most versified bird in Western literature. To medieval French troubadours and German minnesingers, nightingales were emblems of spring and of love, both courtly and bawdy. In the thirteenth century

11

they came to stand for the dawning mood of liberal humanism against the authoritarianism of the traditional Church, for festiveness against puritanism. For early English writers, too, they were cheerful, engaging birds, the friends and confidants of lovers. In much of Renaissance Europe 'listening to the nightingale' became a euphemism for sexual frolicking.

Then, for a few centuries, the mood changed. Influenced by a group of maudlin classical myths which had only a tangential connection with the real bird, pastoral poets began representing the nightingale's song as an outpouring of grief. Matthew Arnold's verse was one of the last gasps of this tradition, but also one of the most mawkish: 'That wild, unquench'd, deep-sunken, old-world pain . . . /How thick the bursts come crowding through the leaves!/Again – thou hearest!/Eternal passion!/Eternal Pain!'

But by this time the bird had already been recaptured by the Romantics, and become the subject of three of the great poems of the era – by Coleridge, Keats and Clare. Each gave a quite different gloss to the song, but all three were inspired by real nightingales, and in their separate ways were united in a celebration of what they saw as the birds' joyous affirmation of life.

It has been a heavy burden of symbolism for a small bird to bear, and countless nightingales were all too literally sacrificed for it. In the age of sympathetic magic ('like cures like'), their organs were used in love potions and in nostrums for improving the voice. In 1661 Robert Lovell recommended the bird's flesh as a remedy for sleepiness: 'The *flesh* is sweete and wholesome. It causeth watchfulnesse . . . The *gall* with honey cleareth the eyes.'

But the bird had more benign ways of encouraging watchfulness. Naturalists listened to it, observed its comings and goings, and had their own insights. In the seventeenth century, it provided the evidence for the first theory linking bird song with nesting territory – and, three cen-

turies later, for the realisation that such elaborate performances must stand for a good deal more.

On occasions it has made whole parishes hold their
breath for a season. The writer Garth Christian remem-
bered a time in the 1930s when a stray pair were reported
in the Golden Valley in Derbyshire, way outside their
usual range. They were treated like prodigies:

> For a night or two the excitements of whippet racing
> and pigeon fancying were forgotten. Men listened
> earnestly and critically as they did when the parish
> choir performed *The Messiah*. Short tough colliers
> who had worked with D.H. Lawrence ('T'a young
> lad of 'is were a rum 'n, all brain an' not a deal of
> muscle'), men who shared a deep delight in Handel
> and strong beer, and real pride in the bullfinches
> they kept in tiny cages, crowded along the lane
> where the nightingale sang.

In Yorkshire an even more exceptional pair became such
a local attraction that an enterprising bus firm started a
'Nightingale Special', ferrying passengers to the wood at
sixpence a head. And in the 1920s, the Metropolitan Railway Company, attempting to create the first generation
of commuters, focused one of its advertising campaigns
around the bird's comforting presence at the end of the
line:

> The song of the nightingales for which the
> neighbourhood is renowned; its gentle pastures,
> woods and streams; its gentle hills clothed with
> verdure, created by crops and thicket; the network
> of translucent rivers traversing the valley, render
> Rickmansworth a Mecca to the city man pining for
> country and pure air.

No wonder that other nocturnal singers are often trans-
figured into nightingales in the minds of hopeful listeners.
Robins, for example (the most common 'false night-

ingales'), are apt to break into wistful song at any time of night and any time of year, especially in the warmth of towns. It may well have been a suburban robin that William Cowper, normally a perceptive observer of birds, described in his poem 'To the Nightingale, which the Author heard Sing on New Year's Day': 'Whence is it that, amazed, I hear/From yonder withr'd spray/This foremost morn of all the year,/The melody of May?' (Nightingales sing in the daytime too, but are 6000 miles away from Britain on New Year's Day.) And the night birds which have made Londoners pause in their strolls through Berkeley Square ever since Judy Campbell first sang the famous song at the height of the Blitz in 1940 have all been insomniac robins or blackbirds.

But why the nightingale? Why *not* the robin or blackbird, or one of the summer warblers? They all have captivating songs, yet none of them has become such a source of inspiration and metaphor. Is the appeal of the nightingale's song simply self-fulfilling, with one generation of romantic associations and literary references shaping the next? Or does it have some intrinsic quality, some deep structure that reaches sympathetic depths in us?

It hardly needs spelling out that one source of the birds' power is their association with the night, and a way of life that seems imbued with secrecy. Their song apart, nightingales are among the least public of birds. They are subfusc, retiring and temporary. They come to Europe for just a few months each spring and sing for not much more than six weeks. This virtual disembodiment has helped make their song the equivalent of a psychologist's ink-blot test, capable of carrying all kinds of meaning, and has heightened its ambivalence. It is only a bird song, yet is undeniably musical and expressive, and seems to involve something close to aesthetic choice on the part of the bird. And in touching us emotionally it begins to stray over that crucial line by which we separate ourselves (and our supposedly unique gifts) from the rest of creation.

Oscar Wilde's poignant children's story 'The Nightingale and the Rose' hinges partly on this possibility, and on the question of whether a bird song can be regarded as being on a par with human art. It also gathers together many of the images and conundrums that surround the bird. At its base is a widespread myth that first appears in early Iranian poetry, of a nightingale heightening the passion of its song by pressing its breast against a thorn, sometimes until it dies. (A stanza by the Iranian poet Hafiz goes: 'The nightingale with drops of his heart's blood/Had nourished the red rose, then came a wind/And catching at the boughs in envious mood,/A hundred thorns about his heart entwined.')

In Wilde's story, the hero (for want of a better word) is a young philosophy student. He is languishing for a professor's daughter, who says she will dance with him at a ball if he brings her a red rose. But, he bewails, 'in all my garden there is no red rose.' A nightingale hears the student crying, and marvels.

'Here, indeed, is the true lover,' it says. 'What I sing of, he suffers: what is joy to me, to him is pain.' The bird decides to help but, on consulting the trees in the garden, finds that this will only be possible at a terrible cost. The rose tree, damaged by frost and gales, says that it can grow a red rose, but the nightingale 'must sing to me with your breast against a thorn. All night you must sing to me, and the thorn must pierce your heart, and your life-blood flow into my veins, and become mine.'

'Death is a great price to pay for a red rose,' the bird cries, but 'Love is better than Life, and what is the heart of a bird compared to the heart of a man?' So it resolves on its course of self-sacrifice and sings a farewell song for the oak tree in the garden, which is especially fond of the bird: 'I shall feel lonely when you are gone,' the oak remarks sadly.

The student overhears this performance and afterwards scribbles a criticism in his notebook. 'She [sic – poetic nightingales are often female] has form,' he says to himself, as he walks away through the grove, 'that cannot be denied to her; but has she got feeling? I am afraid not. In fact, she is like most artists; she is all style without any sincerity. She would not sacrifice herself for others. She thinks merely of music, and everybody knows that the arts are selfish. Still, it must be admitted that she has some beautiful notes in her voice. What a pity it is that they do not mean anything, or do any practical good!'

That night, under the moon, the nightingale flies to the rose tree and sings its heart out. And as it dies, so a single, exquisite red rose blooms on the tree.

'What a wonderful piece of luck,' cries the student. 'It is so beautiful that I am sure it has a long Latin name.' He picks the rose and carries it off to the professor's daughter. Alas, she rejects it. The colour will clash with her dress. Besides, the Chamberlain's nephew has already claimed her with a gift of red jewels. The rejected student storms off, hurls the rose into the gutter (where a cart runs over it) and returns to his books: 'What a silly thing Love is . . . it is always telling one of things that are not going to happen, and making one believe things that are not true . . . I shall go back to Philosophy and study Metaphysics.'

The twist Wilde gives to this story turns on its head one of the mainstays of bad Romantic writing: the idea that human emotions are sympathetically reflected in the natural world (the so-called Pathetic Fallacy). In Wilde's story, nature, in the shape of the nightingale, suffers by believing its hopes and feelings are reflected in *human* behaviour.

Wilde probably had other purposes in his story. Yet that shift of focus, from bird back to human, does open up a new way of looking at the mystery of the nightingale's appeal, and at what kind of communication is going on when we listen to its song. Most of the imaginative answers to this conundrum have been human-centred, and in essence have sought ways in which singing nightingales resemble humans. They have looked at how closely the song approximates to music, at its capacity for absorbing – and conjuring up – memories and associations, at its power as a metaphor. Yet as far back as the medieval period there was another strand of writing which saw humans (poets and lovers especially) as a kind of nightingale.

These days this viewpoint at least has more ecological respectability. It suggests, for instance, that the singing bird may be a kind of cultural ancestor, stirring primordial musical instincts, or ancient, common biological responses to place and season. It may even hint at a modern meaning for Romanticism, not in the patently absurd belief that nature feels human emotions, but that, at a basic level, all creatures share expressive feelings about the great pulses of their lives.

from
The Owl and the Nightingale

For when a man has finished the deed,
All his boldness begins to fade.
Once he has stung beneath the dress,
Then his love no longer lasts.
And so it is with your own mood:
As soon as you have started to brood,
Your song goes sour, your tune awry,
For you behave in the self-same way:
When you are done with all your vices,
Your voice begins to go to pieces.
But when the nights come hard and fast,
And bring the freezing winter frost,
Then for the first time it is seen
Who is active, who is keen.
When days are bitter, then you find
Who goes forth, who lags behind . . .

. . . Besides, you're filthy dark and small
Like a sort of sooty ball.
You have no loveliness or strength
And lack harmonious breadth and length.

Some of the Owl's arguments, early 13th
century

3

'A sort of sooty ball'

The real bird behind this labyrinth of associations seems subdued to the point of disproportion. It is a cousin of the robin and little more than six inches long. Its plumage is largely brown, dull buff on the underparts, with a russet back that becomes almost chestnut on the tail. It may not even be a very ancient species, and probably evolved separately from its closest relative, the thrush-nightingale, no more than 20,000 years ago. Now it breeds across the warmer parts of Europe and central Asia, from Portugal and North Africa in the west to Mongolia in the east, with southern Denmark marking its most northerly outpost.

Its breeding range is influenced by climate, and it is more or less confined to areas where the mean July temperature lies between 17 and 30°C. In Britain this means that nightingales have never nested in any numbers north of a line between Yorkshire and Dorset, and rarely above an altitude of about 600 feet. There are no records at all of breeding in west Wales, Ireland, or, unassisted, in Scotland. (Though in the mid-nineteenth century, Sir John

Sinclair tried unsuccessfully to introduce them by filling robins' nests with eggs pilfered from the London area. The young nightingales hatched, flew to Africa in autumn and never came back.)

Their sensitivity to temperature isn't easily explained by their food preferences, as it is with some summer migrants. They take very few aerial insects (many of which only fly when the weather is warm) and feed instead largely on the ground, taking ants, small beetles and occasional spiders, worms and moth larvae. In late summer they will eat fruit, especially wild strawberries and elderberries. They are essentially foragers and move about the undergrowth in long hops, pausing frequently and tilting their heads on one side to listen for prey, in the same engaging way as robins.

They build their nests low in the bush layer, too, usually in a tangle of twigs and shoots, and rarely more than a foot above the ground. The nest seems like an extension of the undergrowth and is woven out of dry grass, some moss and feathers, and quantities of dead leaves, especially oak leaves. The nest-building is done exclusively by the female, who is also responsible for incubating the four or five speckled blue eggs. This leaves the male free to concentrate on territorial singing. But as soon as the young are hatched (in about thirteen days) he joins in feeding them and virtually ceases to sing. The only noises normally heard from nightingales after this are the rather undignified raspberries that serve as their alarm call, and which are also uttered from deep cover.

They are distributed widely across Europe and Asia, though their native habitat always includes dense scrub. In the Netherlands, they haunt the coastal sand dunes and the willow carr around the polders. In southern Russia, they breed in open hornbeam and alder woods and thickets of sea-buckthorn. The Asian race frequents orchards with little more than rough grass growing under the trees. In southern Spain they are common in corkoak scrub, and in bramble and heather clumps in open pinewoods.

The warmer the conditions, the less fussy they are about their habitat. In the Mediterranean area there is almost no kind of vaguely bushy growth in which they don't occur. I have heard them in tiny village gardens in Majorca, on the edges of remote hillside meadows in Crete, and in Provence almost everywhere: in maquis on dry hillsides, in patches of giant reed and tamarisk at the edge of the Camargue rice-fields, in vineyard windbreaks and vineyards gone wild. No one knows the world population, but there are more than a million pairs in France alone.

Nightingales also choose deep cover to sing from, though occasionally they will climb up to an exposed branch. (I once rather unkindly egged a nightingale into a very public declamation by playing its own song back to it from a tape recorder. It climbed to the top of a hawthorn twig to sing, so that I could watch the opening and shutting of its bill, which seemed in no way co-ordinated with the notes that were emerging from it.) As well as their full-blooded territorial recitals, most often delivered at night, they have shorter daytime songs aimed at approaching rivals, quiet courtship songs and more fragmentary calls for contacting the hen bird inside their territory, which say, it seems, 'Here I am. Where are you?'

In 1929 an English ornithologist watched a male at close quarters for more than a week. 'I have never seen a bird so brimful of emotion,' he wrote. 'On the day the young hatched the male only brought food. Each time he visited his brooding mate he sang such a song as I had never heard before. His beak was full of juicy grubs for the family but this did not hinder him from pouring out a stream of liquid bubbling notes so soft and sweet that they were inaudible six feet away.'

The full territorial songs can sometimes turn into marathon performances. One bird was recorded as singing for twenty-three and a half hours in a single day. Separate spells of singing usually last between five and thirty minutes and are broken up into phrases of two to four seconds, with slightly shorter silences between. The phrases are hugely diverse (individual birds may have many hundreds in their vocabulary), but are always roughly similar in structure. There is a flourish of piping notes to begin with, sometimes in triplets or short arpeggios, and often with an urgent, whiplash quality; then a single note repeated as a rich, liquid bubbling or chuckling or slow trill, which in different phrases occurs at different pitches and speeds. The most extreme variation on this structure is so distinctive as to be almost the bird's signature tune. It is a sequence of long, sighing, indrawn whistles, mounting in crescendo on a single note until they fall, dramatically, to a deep rattle. These are the 'sweet, sweet, sweet, jug, jug' notes of so many poems (Coleridge's for example: 'And murmurs musical and swift jug jug,/And one low piping sound more sweet than all . . .').

Like other birds, it seems as if nightingales are born with an instinctive appreciation of the *kind* of song they ought to sing, its structure, tonality and overall 'jizz' (the quality that makes it possible to identify a bird – or a person for that matter – from a fragment of movement or vocal sound). An individual bird then builds up its vocabulary by listening to its male parent and to other singing males. It may occasionally mimic phrases from other birds, especially blackcaps and thrushes. I have heard an otherwise rather subdued bird in Spain repeat a thrush-like couplet twice, exactly as a song thrush might; and another in Suffolk apparently so pleased with a more conventional nightingale phrase that he ran through it four times in succession. (John Clare once heard the converse of this, a thrush learning phrases from a nightingale: 'the little thrush that commenced singing in april sung till the middle of July & that he had got many variations from the nightingale in the last month which he did not commence

24

with in april.') But this is a scarce occurrence and always has the feel of a deliberate choice by the bird, rather than the kind of occasional repetition that comes from the random shuffling of phrases. If it happened more often, the nightingale might not be regarded as such a 'good' singer.

We are back with the conundrum at the centre of the nightingale's story. The phrase 'good singer' trips off the tongue, but what exactly does it mean? Music is presumed to be a human invention and an *intentional* creation, and it may not be appropriate to use the word for another species. And, for each species, its own song is by definition 'the best' – at least at fulfilling its biological functions.

Yet it is also obvious that sound communication is not qualitatively all of a piece. Voices convey more, in terms of information and emotion, than coincidental natural noise – the sounds of breathing or eating, for instance. Bird calls convey more than the unvarying chirps of insects, and bird *songs*, more than any other communication in the natural world. Caught somewhere between chance euphony – the rustle of a southerly breeze in the trees – and deliberate, abstracted music, they are full of evolutionary possibility. Perhaps they contain within them the template for our own musical sense.

As for the nightingale's song, it has always had for me the extra resonance of *oratory*. It hovers on the edge of speech, of dramatic monologue. And with its crescendos and redolent pauses, the whole performance could, at a pinch, be described as operatic. This is certainly the sense that H.E. Bates caught, in what I think is the most evocative of all prose descriptions of the song:

It has some kind of electric, suspended quality that has a far deeper beauty than the most passionate of its sweetness. It is a performance made up, very often, more of silence than of utterance. The very silences have a kind of passion in them, a sense of breathlessness and restraint, of restraint about to be magically broken. It can be curiously seductive and maddening, the song beginning very often by a sudden low chucking, a kind of plucking of strings, a sort of tuning up, then flaring out in a moment into a crescendo of fire and honey and then, abruptly, cut off again in the very middle of the phrase. And then comes that long, suspended wait for the phrase to be taken up again, the breathless hushed interval that is so beautiful. And often, when it is taken up again, it is not that same phrase at all, but something utterly different, a high sweet whistling prolonged and prolonged for the sheer joy of it, or another trill, or the chuck-chucking beginning all over again.

A Prediction

Our Host had three Nightingales, placed separately, so
that each was shut up singly by itself in a dark Cage. It
happened that at that time, being the Spring of the year,
when those birds are wont to sing indefatigably, and
almost incessantly; I was so afflicted with the Stone, that
I could sleep but very little all night. Then about and
after Midnight, where there was no noise in the house,
but all still, you might have heard strange janglings and
emulations of two Nightingales, talking one with
another, and plainly imitating men's discourses. For my
part I was almost astonished with wonder. For they in
the night-season, when all was whist and quiet, in
conference together produced and repeated whatever
they had heard in the day time from the Guests talking
together, and had thought upon . . . it is wonderful to
tell, how they provoked one another, and by answering
invited and drew one another to speak. Yet did they not
confound their words, talking both together, but rather
utter them alternately, or by course . . . a History or
Prediction of the War of the Emperour against the
Protestants, which was then imminent. For as it were
presaging or prophecying they seemed to chant forth
the whole business as it afterwards fell out. They did also
with that story mingle what had been done before
against the Duke of Brunswick. But I suppose those Birds
had all from the secret conference of some Noblemen
and Captains, which as being in a public Inn, might
frequently have been had in that place where the Birds
were kept.

Gesner, quoted by Francis Willughby, in
The Ornithology, 1628

4

'Most melancholy bird'

Many of the scientific accounts of nightingale songs are oddly distant and reductionist, as if they were describing a string of random morse code signals or a test exercise on a musical instrument. There is no sense that the *structure* of the song might have just as much significance as the vehemence of its delivery. Perhaps this is because many of the nightingales so studied were in cages, which invariably imprison the imagination of the listener as much as they do the bird.

Caged nightingales were popular at least as far back as the Roman empire, and were looked on as a kind of status symbol. Pliny (in 77 AD) remarks that the best singers could fetch the kind of prices normally given for slaves:

> A bird not in the lowest rank remarkable. In the first place there is so loud a voice and so persistent a supply of breath in such a tiny little body; then there is the consummate knowledge of music in a single

bird: the sound is given out with modulations, and now is drawn out into a long note with one continuous breath, now made staccato by checking it, or linked together by prolonging it, or carried on by holding it back; or it is suddenly lowered, and at times sinks into a mere murmur, loud, low, bass, treble, with trills, long notes, modulated when this seems good – soprano, mezzo, baritone; and briefly all the devices in that tiny throat which human science has devised with all the elaborate mechanisms of the flute . . .

Fifteen hundred years later Pliny's fellow-countryman, Olina, became the first naturalist to realise the connection between bird song and assertion of territory. It was, he suggested, 'proper' to the nightingale, 'at his first coming to occupy or seize upon one place as its freehold, into which it will not admit any other nightingale but its mate'. He was, as it turned out, quite correct. But his scientific credibility on this point was hardly helped by the fact that he occasionally rooted birds to the spot with an 'odoriferous unguent':

> As the Nightingale exceeds all other birds in singing, so doth he also in the exquisiteness of his scent.

So,

> Take of Civet not sophisticate twenty grains, Benjamin and Storax calamite, of each three grains, mingle these together in a Mortar in the form of an ointment; Then diligently observe the bush and particular branch, on which the Nightingale is wont to sit and sing, and there making as it were a little shelf of the leaves and boughs, lay thereon four meal-worms, and anoint the branch next to your shelf with this Unguent. The Nightingale when he returns from feeding, will presently fly up to his bough, and finding there the meal-worms will fall a

eating of them, and senting the odour of the
Ointment will begin to sing, and being as it were
intoxicated with the perfume, will not give over, nor
stir from the place though you take the boughs from
about him.

Even eighteenth-century naturalists had few qualms about
catching the birds. Daines Barrington, one of Gilbert
White's correspondents, had the renowned surgeon John
Hunter dissect large numbers of songbirds and discovered
that those with the 'best' voices had the strongest and
most developed larynxes. The nightingale's was larger
than that of any bird of comparable size. The popular
natural history painter Eleazar Albin had a seemingly more
tender attitude, and was fulsome in his praise of bird
musicianship. In *A Natural History of British Song-birds*
(1737) he writes:

> The Animal World does not afford more agreeable
> Objects to the Eyes, nor none that so sweetly
> gratifies the Sense of Hearing. They were
> undoubtedly designed by the Great Author of
> Nature, on Purpose to entertain and delight
> Mankind, who for their Generosity are well pleased
> with these pretty inocent Creatures.

But he was also a creature of his time, and couldn't see
beyond the image of songbirds as divine toys for human
entertainment. He continues:

> I could not do a more acceptable service for the
> Lovers of these sweet Choristers of the Woods, than
> to instruct how to catch and keep them.

His instructions on procuring and training reliable dom-
estic nightingales are a long way removed from his earlier
blandishments. He insists that they should be taken before

they have fledged. They should be fed with 'sheep's Heart, or other Flesh Meat raw, chopped very fine . . . well cleansed and freed from Skin, sinews, and Fat or Strings, which will be apt to stick in their Throats, or twine about their Tongues . . . .' He reckoned they could become 'fat and foggy' in autumn (when they should be fed spiders) and 'gouty' if kept for long periods in a cage.

John Bingley, in *Animal Biography* (1802), went one stage further in praising the accomplishments of the 'Choristers of the Woods'. He drew up a league table of the 'comparative merits of the singing-birds of our own island', scored as if they were competing in a village show. He awarded seventeen species marks out of twenty for five qualities. The nightingale wins, scoring nineteen for 'mellowness of tone', fourteen for 'sprightliness', and nineteen each for 'plaintiveness', 'compass' and 'execution'. The robin was awarded respectively 6, 16, 12, 12, 12, and the linnet 12, 16, 12, 16, 18. There are some curious anomalies in Bingley's list, symptoms perhaps of the taste of the times. The blackbird's languorous song, for instance, wins just four for mellowness and nothing at all for plaintiveness; and the dunnock's, which these days would be regarded as one of the most cheerful of hedgerow jingles, gets nought for sprightliness.

Bingley was another keeper of caged nightingales and he passes on stories of the quirks and performances he has either heard or heard about. If humans play or sing to them they can be taught to whistle in tune or in time and will spontaneously modulate their key if necessary. They can even be persuaded to join in 'choruses . . . and to repeat their couplet at the proper time'.

The life expectations (and probably the songs) of the majority of hapless nightingales caught to adorn bird-fanciers' parlours were dismal. In 1867 James Harting logged the bags of three professional catchers in outer London, and found that between 13 April and 2 May they took 225 birds, all but six of them male. The techniques of the

trappers who used to loot the Surrey woods (then believed
to house the best songsters) were described in grisly detail
by Richard Jefferies in 1886:

> In the 'good old days of bird-catching' it was child's
> play to snare them. A couple of roughs would come
> down from town and silence a whole grove. The
> nightingale would watch the trap being laid, and
> pounce on the alluring meal-worm as soon as the
> trapper was out of sight. It would be quite as much
> curiosity as gluttony that led to its fate; and the fate
> was a sad one. These birds are so shy that it is nearly
> impossible to keep them alive. They literally beat
> themselves to death against their prison wires. So
> for the first fortnight of captivity the wings were tied,
> and the bird was kept caged in the dark. Light was
> gradually let in – at first by a few pinholes in the
> paper that covered the cage. The captive would peck
> and peck at these until a rent was made and in time
> the paper could come away. The mortality was
> pitiable. Seventy percent of these little creatures that
> were singing a week before in full-throated ease in
> the Surrey lanes would be flung out into the gutters
> of Seven Dials or Whitechapel.

A succession of bird protection acts, beginning in 1880,
has largely put a stop to this sordid trade. But nightingales
are still caught and reared in captivity, and still experi-
mented with. In 1992 two behavioural zoologists at the
Free University of Berlin caught and isolated nightingale
nestlings and then 'tutored' them by playing tapes of bird
song. They found that the birds could often repeat complex sequences of up to sixty different phrases after hearing them once a day for two or three weeks. During the
experiment they discovered a good deal about how nightingales learned new material and stored it in different
memory layers. (Their short-term memory alone can
accommodate seven song sequences, each nearly a minute
long.)

The remarkable story of the ventriloquial nightingales, quoted at the beginning of this chapter, was recounted by the seventeenth-century ornithologist Francis Willughby. It concerned an experience of a friend of the German scientist Gesner, who was attending the Diet at Ratisbone in 1546, and staying at 'a common Inn at the sign of the Golden Crown'. The narrator is sceptical at first of the birds' facility for 'imitating men's discourses', and asks his host whether the birds' tongues have been slit, or if they have been deliberately taught. The host answers no, and denies any knowledge of the birds' nocturnal conversations. But the guest, not able to sleep because of his illness, continues to be entertained by the birds' apparent gossip. He hears tales of the continuing rows between a tapster and his wife, repeated in all their original, unexpurgated detail ('And if by chance in their wrangling they cast forth any unseemly words, and that ought rather to have been suppressed and kept secret, the Birds, not knowing the difference between modest and immodest, honest and filthy words, did out with them.') And, most bizarrely, they also uttered 'a History or Prediction of the War of the Emperour against the Protestants, which was then imminent'. (Charles V declared war on 26 June 1546.)

It is hard to understand what was really going on during those nights at Ratisbone. Perhaps the whole thing was just the fantasy of an ill and possibly intoxicated insomniac. Perhaps, like Keats's Ruth, he was also 'sick for home'. Or perhaps the narrator was making a veiled political or religious point. Given the nightingale's reputation as a catalyst for the imagination, it might even be an early urban myth.

A Riddle

I talk through my mouth with many tongues,
Vary my tone, and often change
The sound of my voice. I give loud cries,
Keep my tune, make songs without ceasing.
An old evening singer, I bring pleasure
To people in towns. When I burst
Into a storm of notes, they fall silent,
Suddenly listening. Say what I'm called
Who like a mimic loudly mock
A player's song, and announce to the world
Many things that are welcome to men.

Anon, probably 8th century

5

'The happiest part of summers
fame . . .'

The nightingale's song is so hedged about with associations that it is hard to say if there is anything intrinsically captivating about it. Did it turn the heads of prehistoric humans? Do young children notice it, unprompted? I have no recollection of hearing nightingales when I was a child, but suspect I must have done. By all accounts the birds were common enough in the Chiltern woods and heaths I haunted in the late 1940s and '50s. I knew a few birds' songs, especially ones that were rhythmic enough to imitate. I could recognise – and just about whistle back – the green woodpecker's 'yaffle' and the yellowhammer's 'little bit of bread and no cheese'. And, with an excited, half-formed sense that they were portents of the spring, I learned to listen out for the songs of returning warblers. But either the nightingales were somewhere else, or their sophisticated phrases failed to connect with the preoccupations of a juvenile birdwatcher.

Children's responses may depend on the context in

which they hear the bird. When he was little more than five years old, Coleridge's son, Hartley, could already recognise – and apparently relish – the Quantock birds that his father was to celebrate in one of the great nightingale poems.

> *How he would place his hand beside his ear,*
> *His little hand, the small forefinger up,*
> *And bid us listen!*

The young son of my East Anglian friend Roger Deakin also benefited from his father's enthusiasm for the bird. When he was seven years old he read Roald Dahl's story *Danny the Champion of the World* and developed a desperate desire to try his hand at poaching. Roger, not wanting to squash his interest, suggested they hunted nightingales with a tape recorder rather than pheasants with a gun, and they spent an enchanted night together in the Suffolk woods. (When he was much older Roger's son returned the compliment by 'arranging' the song they recorded that night as part of an answerphone message.)

The young Gertrude Jekyll, on the other hand, became tetchy about the sheer volume of nightingale song that anyone living in the Surrey woods was subject to in the nineteenth century. One morning, when she was in her early teens, she came down to breakfast without boots. Asked by her parents to explain, she said she had hurled them at the nightingales carolling ceaselessly outside her bedroom.

Max Ernst's surrealist picture-relief 'Two Children are Threatened by a Nightingale' (1924) relies for much of its effect on the benign, or at least ingenuous, views children normally have of the bird: only in the most disorientating kind of dream could a nightingale possibly seem *threatening*. But Ernst's piece is precisely of a dream full of irrationality and menace. Across a landscape hemmed in by a wall, two figures flee from a hovering nightingale no bigger than a speck in the vast sky. A girl, holding what seems to be a dagger in her hand, is running either towards the bird or towards a wooden gate which is hinged to the frame of the work. A male figure, holding another small girl in his arms, leaps along the roof of a tiny, windowless house. He is reaching out into the real world, towards an alarm bell, which is also fixed to the frame. A fourth figure lies prostrate by the side of the house.

It is a disrupted and unsettling picture, but would be equally so if the 'threatening' creature were a wren or a butterfly. Given that the Freudian theory of dreams was one of the chief inspirations of surrealism, the deliberate naming of the minute bird in Ernst's picture as a nightingale may be a reference to its tradition as a symbol – and inciter – of sexual liaisons.

But that is one of the more sophisticated nightingale associations, and a comparatively late arrival in the bird's cultural history – just as it is in most listeners' lives. For most of us, I suspect, the songs of particular birds stand for more homely and personal memories. They can be as evocative as smells for conjuring up places, holidays, friendships, love affairs and, especially, moments of the year. An early blackbird song, for instance, can still summon up for me the mood and character of a particular moment in my childhood. It is an early evening in late March, the clocks have just been put forward and there is a warm southerly breeze. It is the first day our back door is left open after tea, joining the house with the garden again. And soon I am sitting out there, listening to the rambling monologues from the tops of the garden trees.

If the blackbird's song was the first I remember, the swift's was the first I deliberately sought out. From May onwards the packs screamed round the school hall and the parish church where our choir sang motets through the summer. They were good-luck charms for me, and I used to trudge up to cricket at the start of the summer term, clutching my blazer collar and fervently hoping that I would catch my first glimpse of those careering crescent wings on the first day of May.

When, a little older, I became a more serious birdwatcher, the chiffchaff was another talisman, and its song a sure sign that the Easter holidays had begun. But the ritual of combing the local woods for the first arrival was as much a competitive game as a celebration of spring, and my chief aim was to push my personal date as far as possible back into March. I had read somewhere that the first waves of migrants reached this country 'as promptly as if they were following an airline timetable'. Chiffchaffs came on 16 March, followed by willow warblers on the 21st. I was amazed at the thought of these diminutive creatures making their 5000-mile journeys with such precision, and longed to hear one on its 'proper' date.

Even then there was something that touched me about the chiffchaff's optimistic, see-saw note, drifting down from the top of a leafless ash tree. I soon realised that chiffchaffs were individuals and did not all sound like metronomes. Their songs were often relaxed, loose-rhythmed, slurred. I heard one bird which always sang a pure triplet – chiff-*chaff*-chiff; another whose song was pared down to a minimalist chiff-chiff.

In late autumn the first fieldfare flocks would arrive from Scandinavia. I would often hear them, sounding like the clacking of distant castanets, as they passed high overhead in the early morning; or late in a November afternoon, shuttling in invisible, nomadic bands through the gathering mist. Without fail their southerly flights were followed within two or three days by the first bad weather of the winter.

Much later in my life, bird songs began to be emblems for particular habitats. The bubbling sound of the curlew still conjures up Yorkshire Dales hay-meadows in May, and the piping three-note whistle of the greenshank, as pure and powerful in its own way as the opening bars of a nightingale's song, the Norfolk marshes in late summer. The scratches and churrs of grasshopper warblers, turtle doves, nightjars and whitethroats seem perfectly suited to the scruffy, spiny cover of their favourite heathland habitats. The whitethroat's bramble-patch style even extends to its song flight, which Gilbert White described as a series of 'odd jerks and gesticulations over the hedges and bushes'.

I understood just how deeply these songs were impacted with particular places when, one summer when I was in my early thirties, they began to fade. I thought at first that there had simply been another warbler slump, until I realised the swift packs were also silent and that almost all other birds seemed to have receded into the distance. I had, it turned out, premature high-tone hearing loss. Fortunately it has remained stable and selective. I doubt if I will hear swifts or crickets again, or the flourish at the end of a wren's song, or, unassisted, the full tumult of a dawn chorus. But a modern hearing aid has restored virtually everything else and brought, thank goodness, the blackbirds back into the garden.

I think this experience, of the loss of what amounted to part of my sense of place, may have been responsible for an odd, compensatory belief I nurtured for a while. So many bird songs seemed to me to 'fit' a landscape, to be scored as evocatively as pieces of programme music, that I began to suspect it was an ecological adaptation, the sound equivalent of camouflage. Put like that, of course, it was an absurd, anthropomorphic fantasy: landscape 'character' is a human construct which bird song helps to shape, rather than being shaped by it.

Yet there may have been a grain of truth in my theory. Birds which frequent similar habitats do have similar qualities in their songs and calls. Birds of open spaces, for example, can rely on visual signals and convey messages

41

by plumage or display flights. Their songs tend to be short and uncomplicated. Birds of dense woodland, on the other hand, need to place more emphasis on sound for communication and advertisement, and their songs are often elaborate and far-reaching. This seems to hold true whether the wood in question is a rain forest or an English copse. Edward Armstrong, an ornithologist at Cambridge, has given a graphic account of how he was struck by homesickness on hearing the bird songs of the Amazonian jungle.

> The clanging note of the bell-bird of the South American forest stirs the emotions – for a moment the surprised wayfarer is transported by the bell-note out of the wilderness to the Sunday calm of an English hamlet. Almost simultaneously, conscious of the enveloping rain forest, disillusionment and a sense of desolation assail him.

Nightingales came into my life rather late, at a time when I was more interested in adding new birds to my list than in looking for romantic associations. My first encounter with the bird was in such incongruous circumstances as to be almost comic. I was up on the north Norfolk coast in the late '60s, rediscovering birdwatching with an old friend. We had spent most of our time down on the salt-marshes, poking about in the creeks and watching the spring passage of wading birds en route from Africa to their breeding grounds. It was a feast of first encounters for us: black-tailed godwits mobbing Montagu's harriers, ruffs in such gaudily varied summer plumage that we thought they were all different species, and urgent flocks of dunlin and golden plover, bound for the northern tundra. We made shameless lists – of first-time birds, birds seen in a day, birds *possibly* seen.

One morning we struck inland on the trail of the red-backed shrikes that nested regularly on a stretch of heathland half a mile from the coast. We knew roughly where they were to be found, in a patch of thorn scrub by a grassy clearing that served as a parking space. We duly parked the car and waited. The day was drab and overcast, and there was no sign of the shrikes. Robins and willow warblers tried out brief, fitful phrases and then fell silent. It was the kind of day for moping in a bush, or a car. But just before noon, out of the blackthorn – though seemingly out of nowhere – came a burst of glass-clear notes that jolted us out of our torpor. Neither of us had heard a nightingale before, but we knew instantly what it must be. It was the power and tone of the song that was so striking. It seemed ridiculously loud for this little heath-land enclave, almost theatrically projected, as if a migrant wader from the marsh had set down in a bush and begun calling for company.

Soon this first bird was joined by a second, singing from the opposite side of the clearing, and for twenty minutes we sat enthralled while they duelled across us, swapping phrases, shouting each other down, at times linked in what seemed like a musical round. And as potent as the phrases themselves were the cliff-hanging silences that punctuated them, and which I was to learn were one of the key elements of the bird's performance, as if it were deliberately leaving space for a reply.

I heard and remember all this, but cannot recall being stirred to passion or melancholy or any of the emotions supposedly aroused by, or contained in, the nightingale's song. All I recollect about my reactions when that first stream of notes flared out is erupting with a rash of sym-pathetic gooseflesh. I rated the bird as a very collectable tick, and thought the whole performance, at that unprom-ising spot and time, an incongruously choice experience, like taking an exotic cocktail with elevenses.

I didn't come across many more nightingales for the next few years, but that Norfolk experience proved to be more than a chance meeting. I soon realised that, in East

Anglia at least, the birds had a particular liking for dense scrub near grassy clearings, and I became a connoisseur of rural car-park performers. It grew to be something of a party trick. I would draw up nonchalantly in a likely lay-by in May or early June, bet myself or my companion that a nightingale was there and simply wait for it to start up. I usually won my bet, though I am not terribly proud to admit it. I think I did pick up a vague and instinctive sense of the kind of place nightingales haunted (and a knack of identifying their song a long way off from just a couple of notes). But these auditions were really just showing off, a kind of territorial display of my own, and it was years before I found any subtler resonances in the song. In those early days the nightingale's song simply meant the open heaths, the English bush and those enticingly warm, muddled scrublands of the south country.

The bush may be the oldest association of all, and perhaps the bird's aboriginal home. At the height of the most recent ice age, nightingales may not have been migratory birds. They may have spent the whole year in the savanna, the open scrubland which then covered much of the African continent. But as the ice retreated from northern Europe, the African interior began to warm up and it is possible that this prompted the regular seasonal escapes to more bearable temperatures that eventually became the habit of migration. The nightingale arrived in Britain, to judge from the few fossils that have been found, about 10,000 years ago.

It is hard to imagine them being ignored by early people in northern Europe. They were key players in the great annual change-around of birds each spring. One week there would be flocks of wild duck and geese on the wetlands, and the next packs of swifts screaming round the crags and countless small birds piping in the undergrowth. More often than not, the arrival of these summer migrants would coincide with spells of fine weather, and they must have been looked on as good omens.

Even then, nightingales would have stood out as something remarkable, the loudest and most tantalisingly secretive of the newcomers. Did people try to mimic them, hoping that, by sympathetic magic, a few reverently echoed phrases might guarantee more of those hunters' moons under which the song was so often heard?

It is also likely that nightingales were already a kind of village familiar at this time, drawn to the edges of human settlements for the bushy, open woodland that is their favoured nesting habitat. In truly natural conditions (in northern Europe, at least) this kind of scrub woodland is quite scarce. It was abundant just after the retreat of the ice, but the climate then was too cool for there to be any nightingales to enjoy it. And when the temperatures did improve and the climax forest became established, scrub largely retreated to open, disturbed areas like flood-plains. It would flourish for a while where big trees had died and fallen, or where there had been forest fires, but vanish again as the woodland regenerated.

It was the arrival of the first farmers that gave scrub its big boost. By clearing woodland for settlements and regularly and deliberately cropping trees to provide building materials and fuel (a practice which had almost certainly begun by 4000 BC in Britain), they created exactly the kind of bushy regrowth that has perennially attracted nightingales.

This was an association that flourished for as long as the practice of coppicing itself remained the common way of managing woodland. Coppicing relies on the ability of most of our native deciduous trees to sprout sheaves of bushy new poles if they are regularly cut back to ground level. Woods were usually cut on a rotation of between ten and fifteen years (chiefly to supply a continuous crop of firewood) and during cuts the compartments developed into dense shrubberies. As a commercial practice, coppicing became largely obsolete in Britain after the Second World War, though increasing numbers of old coppices are being revived for nature conservation or amenity reasons.

But nightingales don't use coppice woods indiscriminately. A survey in Kent at the beginning of the 1970s showed that their concentrations reach a peak five to eight years after the coppice is cut and fall away dramatically after ten years. Many similar studies since, in Suffolk, Essex, Oxfordshire and Worcestershire, for instance, have confirmed this finding. Nightingales like the density of vegetation in middle-aged coppicewood. It is tall and thick enough to provide good cover, but not so dark that the lower undergrowth – of honeysuckle and bramble perhaps – is shaded out. They also seem to prefer an intimate mix of coppice species – ash, maple, hazel and oak, for example – and a scatter of uncut, standard trees amongst the bushy underwood. This may be because such trees provide denser areas of leaf-litter for feeding, or because low, tangled vegetation can persist for longer under their dappled shade than under the very dark cover of mature coppice.

But there is much that is still mysterious about nightingales' habitat preferences. They will not nest regularly, for instance, in coppices where less than about seven to eight acres is cut each year. In some woods they will nest in free-growing areas and ignore the regularly cut plots. The pattern of their retreat from England echoes, but is in no way precisely correlated with, the pattern of the decline of coppicing. And the reinstatement of coppicing at former nesting sites does not guarantee that nightingales will return. It may be that they have a strong loyalty to traditional nesting spots and won't colonise new areas readily, especially when these are some way from the places in which they were hatched and reared. Or perhaps that larger trends in climate are influencing the birds, particularly during migration. In recent years they have had to run the gauntlet of African droughts, exceptional spring storms and frosts in the Mediterranean and capricious weather in England itself, all of which may have affected them in ways more subtle than the simple availability of prey.

Song

Sweet Philomell in groaues and desarts haunting,
Oft glads my hart and eares with her sweet chaunting,
  But then her tunes delight me best,
  When percht with prick against her breast,
She sings fie, fie, fie, fie, as if she suffered wrong
Till seeming pleased sweet, sweet concludes her song.

Sweet Jinny sings and talkes and sweetly smileth,
And with her wanton mirth my griefs beguileth:
  But then me thinkes she pleaseth best,
  When, while my hands move loues request,
She cries phy, phy, phy, phy! and seeming loath
                      gainsaies,
Till better pleased sweet, sweet content bewrayes.

Anon, 16th century

Set by Robert Jones, *The First Book of Songs or Ayres*, 1600

6

'The voluptuous nightingales . . .'

The idea of 'the bush' – the thicket, the secret trysting ground, the hidden retreat – runs like a leitmotif through the nightingale's story. It is one of the natural links between the bird's ecology and its place in romantic poetry, paralleling its real and metaphorical associations with the spring (incidentally an old English word for a bushy coppice).

But as far back as classical times, literary nightingales have been carriers of ideas which don't obviously echo features of the real bird's life. Paramountly they have been birds of love and passion – platonic, flirtatious, promiscuous love and, especially, rejected or hopeless love. To some extent this symbolism may have been fuelled by the 'sobbing' quality which some listeners hear in the song. But its literary origins lie in a widespread and exceptionally grisly classical myth, in which there is a magically 'sympathetic' transformation of a victim of violent dis-tonguing into a bird with wondrous vocal powers.

The myth recounts the fate and metamorphosis of two

sisters, Procne and Philomel. Procne is married to Tereus, king of Thrace, who rapes Philomel and then imprisons her, cutting out her tongue for good measure so that she cannot tell tales. Ovid's version of c. 10 BC is typical of the goriness of this early horror story:

> But he seized her tongue with pincers, as it protested
> against the outrage, calling ever on the name of her
> father and struggling to speak, and cut it off with
> his merciless blade. The mangled root quivers, while
> the severed tongue lies palpitating, faintly
> murmuring; and, as the severed tail of a mangled
> snake is wont to writhe, it twitches to the dark earth
> convulsively, and with its last dying movement it
> seeks its mistress's feet.

Philomel manages to convey the gist of what has happened in a tapestry. The two sisters are reunited and take revenge upon Tereus by killing his son Itys and serving him for dinner. But it is only when Philomel bounds into the room, brandishing the boy's head, that Tereus understands the full horror of his meal. He chases the women through the palace, hoping to kill them, but as they run they turn into birds, Philomel into a nightingale and Procne a swallow (Tereus becomes a hoopoe in some versions, the oddest transformation of the three):

> As they fly from him you would think that the bodies
> of the two Athenians were poised on wings; they
> *were* poised on wings! One flies to the woods, the
> other rises to the roof.

Sanitised of its bloodthirstiness and overt sexual references, the myth's image of love betrayed, and of a nightingale perpetually lamenting this betrayal, was to be reworked in European song and poetry for the next 1800 years. In twelfth-century France and Spain, it was a popular theme of the troubadours and was repeatedly mixed

up with more obvious nightingale associations. In the Provençal language there are some fifty surviving lyrics which
contain references to nightingales. The bird represents, at
various times, the end of winter and the coming of spring,
poetic inspiration, the poet himself, the object of his love,
a medium of communication between lovers and just
occasionally a kind of impish phallic symbol. The famous
anthology of vernacular songs and poems written in Latin
and known as the *Carmina Burana* (probably compiled
about 1230) is full of such versatile birds. Poem 82 ('Fringus
hinc est horridum'), for instance, has Philomel apparently
exorcising her memories in the chorus of spring:

> The hill is clothed with flowers, and resounds from
> the birds; in the woods birds sing together and
> sweetly chatter; nor does *philomena* cease; she
> remembers her loss.

In Poem 179 ('Tempus est iocundum') the poet is being
inflamed by the nightingale's florid song, to the extent
that he begins to see it as a competitor: 'Silence, *philomena*,
for the moment! Rise, song, from my breast! O! O! I am
all aflower!' The last lines may be an early attempt at
echoing the sound of the nightingale's song.

But Latin can't match the resonant and sensuous tones
of Provençal when it comes to celebrating the natural
world, and the nightingale poems of French troubadours
such as Marcabru and Bernard de Ventadour almost all
sound onomatopoeic in performance. Originally, they
were probably delivered as spoken monologues over the
lightest of instrumental backings, and modern reconstruc-
tions in this style, delivered with extravagantly clipped
consonants, drawn-out vowels and theatrical pauses, perhaps come closer than any other kind of music to convey-
ing the atmosphere of a nightingale performance:

> *Bel m'es quan la rana chanta*
> *E.l sucs pueja per la rusca,*

> *Per que.l flors e.l fueilhs e.l busca*
> *E.l frugz reviu en la planta,*
> *E.l rossinnols crid'e brama*
> *Sa par qu'a per joi conquisa,*
> *Ples d'orgueilh car el no sen*
> *Freg ni gel ni glaz ni bisa.*

(Marcabru)

(It pleases me when the frog sings and the sap rises in the bark; because the flowers and the leaves and the branches and the fruit return in the plants and the nightingale cries and calls its mate which it has conquered through joy, filled with pride, for it does not feel cold, nor ice, nor winter wind.)

The Philomel myth was largely abandoned by the later troubadours, yet the nightingale could still remind the poet of his losses in love, because of the contrast between the bird's carefree fluency and the poet's mute melancholy:

> *I do not sleep neither day nor night, for at night,*
> *when I go to bed, the nightingale sings and cries,*
> *and I, who used to sing, die of chagrin and sadness.*

(Bernard de Ventadour)

At the close of the troubadour era in the early thirteenth century, the nightingale appears less often as metaphor. There is an increasing sense (as there is in the representation of nature in the visual arts at this time) that the idea of individuality is being respected, that the nightingale is being seen – and heard – as a creature in its own right, a distinct and different species as well as a part of a common Creation. In a decidedly modernist lyric from about 1205, Peire Cardenal suggests that the one thing that is common to poet and nightingale is that they are both misunderstood by the public:

> I sing and I play the flute for myself, for no man

except me understands my language; the people
understand what my song says as little as they
understand the nightingale. And I do not have a
tongue that shakes or stutters, nor do I know how
to speak Flemish or Angevin, but the meanness
which contains them takes away the vision of what
is false and what is true.

But outside the strict troubadour tradition, nightingales
continued to be a source of ripe imagery. In one of the
tales in *The Decameron*, written by Giovanni Boccaccio
between 1349 and 1351, a young girl, Caterina, wants to
meet her lover, Ricciardo, secretly and asks her parents if
she may go and listen to the nightingales sing ('ludir cantar
l'usignuolo' – a phrase still in use as a bawdy euphemism
in Italy). Caterina's father is either extremely dull or not
taken in at all by her ruse, as he later says to his wife,
'See, your daughter is so crazy for the nightingale that she
has taken it and holds it.'

A more subtle variation on the same idea occurs in Marie
de France's twelfth-century verse romance *Laüstic*. The
story itself echoes many strands of nightingale lore and
tradition. It has sacrifice, a silenced creature, the bird as a
token of frustrated love. It is full of symbolism, at one
extreme being a darkly Freudian parable, at the other a
simple tale of a messenger punished.

A woman from Brittany is married to a respected knight,
but loves another, younger knight who lives close by.
The two are unable to meet, but communicate discreetly,
talking from their neighbouring windows and tossing gifts
to each other. They also commune by listening to the
nightingale which sings between their dwellings. But she
spends so much time at the window, frequently leaving
her bed in the middle of the night, that her husband
becomes angry and asks her repeatedly why she gets up
and where she goes.

'Lord,' she replies, 'anyone who does not hear the song

of the nightingale knows none of the joys of this world. This is why I come and stand here. So sweet is the song I hear by night that it brings me great pleasure. I take such delight in it and desire it so much that I can get no sleep at all.'

On hearing this her husband gives a spiteful laugh and has the nightingale trapped. He takes it to her and says, 'Now you can sleep in peace, for it will never awaken you again.' The lady is grief-stricken; out of spite her husband wrings the bird's neck in front of her and throws the corpse at her, 'so that the front of her tunic was bespattered with blood, just on her breast'. Heartbroken, she places the little body in an embroidered shroud and sends it to the knight. They both understand that their distant affair is over. But the young knight is not 'uncourtly or tardy'. He inters the nightingale in a small gold casket and carries it with him at all times, as a memorial to the dreams they shared.

In Britain, medieval nightingale poetry was by and large more jovial and direct. Anglo-Saxon riddles welcomed the bird back as a cheering harbinger of spring. Dafydd ap Gwilym included 'The brooks songstress . . . Beautiful, slim, sweet-spoken' in his 'Mass of the Grove', even though, as a Welshman, he may never have heard the real thing. In *Troilus and Criseyde*, Chaucer has a nightingale serenade Criseyde to sleep in the moonlight, when she dreams of her lover transformed into a great white eagle.

The greatest English nightingale work of the Middle Ages is the long and often uproarious allegory entitled *The Owl and the Nightingale*. The poem, written about 1225, probably by an associate of Nicholas of Guildford, takes the form of a debate between the two birds, representing the two value systems which were beginning to oppose each other in the medieval world: the ascetic, sin-centred philosophy of traditional Christianity and the emerging ideal of free will and individualism. The owl is solemn and sober, the nightingale joyful and light-hearted. The owl believes in the work ethic, the nightingale in the pleasure principle. The owl is an authoritarian, possibly a conservative, the nightingale a liberal with distinct humanist leanings. For 1794 lines the two birds swap quips and insults. They deprecate each other's appearance, tastes in food, ways of singing. And, despite its underlying seriousness, their debate is carried on with the raciness of a banter between street traders:

> 'Your name is nightingale,' she said,
> 'But chatterbox would do instead,
> Because you're such a gabby pest!
> Let your tongue have a little rest!'

The argument revolves around the birds' respective senses of responsibility and sin. The nightingale sees the owl as full of the miseries of winter and self-restraint, and herself as part of the optimism and joy of spring. ('You sing just like a hen in snow,/And all she sings it is for woe.') The owl, in return, accuses her of encouraging lechery and laziness – and of then running off at the first sign of the privations of winter. She reminds the nightingale of what happened the last time she provoked a wife to adultery (a smear that is a distorted reference to Marie de France's *Laustic*):

> 'And now with low notes, now with high
> You taught her to do shamefully
> And use her body wickedly.
> Her lord found out, before much time,
> And set out traps and spread birdlime
> In hopes he'd catch what caused his shame.
> And click! he had you in his trap,
> And how your shins did feel the snap!'

The nightingale denies that she encourages infidelity. Treachery in relationships is hateful to her, regardless of whether the wife or husband is the guilty party. She would rather encourage true love in a maiden than cruel or heartless relations between married partners.

The argument is not resolved, though the nightingale has marginally the better of it. What the owl disparingingly describes as the nightingale's 'writelinge' – literally 'chirping', but standing one feels for 'chirpiness' in a more general sense – seems by the end of the poem to be a rather good way to approach the travails of life.

From the sixteenth century there was a renaissance of classical verse, and English nightingale poetry began increasingly to revive the myth of Philomel and Procne, and its sister legend of the nightingale singing with its breast against a thorn. Poems from the early part of the sixteenth century cheerfully mix the myths with medieval double entendres about sharp things in the night. John Lyly (c. 1554–1606) talks of the bird's 'Brave prick-song!':

> *What bird so sings, yet so does wail*
> *O tis the ravished nightingale*
> *Jug, jug, jug, tereu, she cries,*
> *And still her woes at midnight rise.*

('Jug' was semi-onomatopoeic slang for the sexual act.)

In Barnabe Barnes (c. 1569–1609) the reference is a shade more explicit: 'I'll sing my Plain Song with the turtle doves/ And Prick Song with the nightingales', and becomes quite unambiguous in the anonymous and saucy 'Song' (c. 1600, see p. 49), and in John Marston's ditty from *The Dutch Courtezan* (1633):

> *The darke is my delight*
> *So tis the Nightingales.*
> *My Musick's in the night,*

> *So is the Nightingales.*
> *My body is but little,*
> *So is the Nightingales.*
> *I love to sleep against prickle*
> *So doth the nightingale.*

Other poems make a more mawkish identification with the abandoned and stricken bird. 'O Philomela fair, O take some gladness,' bewails Sir Philip Sidney (1554–86), 'That here is juster cause of plaintful sadness:/Thine earth now springs, mine fadeth,/Thy thorn without, my thorn my heart invadeth.' Richard Barnfield (1574–1627) admits that 'For her griefs so lively shown/Make me think upon mine own.' Joseph Warton's ode (c. 1745) is addressed to 'Contemplation's favourite bird!':

> *O fail not then, sweet Philomel,*
> *Thy sadly warbled woes to tell;*
> *In sympathetic numbers join*
> *Thy pangs of luckless love with mine!*

At various times, Richard Braithwaite, Patrick Hannay, John Milton, William Blake and Matthew Arnold all composed gushing tributes to the grieving bird. Shelley, surprisingly, was scarcely any better. His allegorical poem, 'The Woodman and the Nightingale', closes with the stanza:

> *The world is full of Woodmen who expel*
> *Love's gentle Dryads from the haunts of love,*
> *And vex the nightingales in every dell.*

And the Semichorus of Spirits from 'Prometheus Unbound' is as indigestible as anything from two centuries before:

> *There the voluptuous nightingales*
> *Are awake through all the broad noonday,*

When one with bliss or sadness fails,
   And through the windless ivy-boughs,
Sick with sweet love droops dying away
   On its mate's music-panting bosom.

But there were isolated writers who stood aside from this
doleful tradition. Cowper (who mistook some other bird
for a nightingale on New Year's Day – see p. 14) redeemed
himself with the delightful 'The Nightingale and the Glow-
worm', in which the worm persuades the bird not to eat
it, out of a kind of workers' solidarity: "twas the self-same
Power Divine/Taught you to sing and me to shine.'

And the most resilient and probably best-known nightingale lyric of all, the folk song titled variously 'The Soldier
and the Lady', 'The Bold Grenadier', or 'The Nightingale',
comes straight out of the medieval tradition of ribald
euphemism. Cecil Sharp heard half a dozen versions of
this on his collecting expeditions in the Southern Appalachian mountains in North America, where they had been
taken by English settlers in the sixteenth century. This
version was recorded in Somerset in 1906, but it could be
matched by lyrics from Carolina or Kentucky:

As I was a-walking one morning in May
I saw a fair young couple as they was walking this way,
O she was a fair maid, a beauty, I declare
And the other was a soldier, a bold grenadier.

Kind kisses and compliments as they both did walk
                                        together
Till they both did come down by the side of some river,
When they sat down together by the clear crystal stream.
Hark, hark, said the fair maid, how the nightingales do
                                        sing.

When he softly clasped his arms all around her middle
And out of his knapsack he pulled out a fiddle.
He played such a tune my boys made the valleys ring.

Hark, hark, said the fair maid, how the nightingales do
sing.

from
The Nightingale. A Conversation Poem

No cloud, no relique of the sunken day
Distinguishes the West, no long thin slip
Of sullen light, no obscure trembling hues.
Come, we will rest on this old mossy bridge!
You see the glimmer of the stream beneath,
But hear no murmuring: it flows silently,
O'er its soft bed of verdure. All is still,
A balmy night! and though the stars be dim,
Yet let us think upon the vernal showers
That gladden the green earth, and we shall find
A pleasure in the dimness of the stars.
And hark! the Nightingale begins its song,
'Most musical, most melancholy' bird!
A melancholy bird? Oh! idle thought!
In nature there is nothing melancholy.
But some night-wandering man whose heart was pierced
With the remembrance of a grievous wrong,
Or slow distemper, or neglected love,
(And so, poor wretch! filled all things with himself,
And made all gentle sounds tell back the tale
Of his own sorrow) he, and such as he,
First named these notes a melancholy strain.
And many a poet echoes the conceit;
Poet who hath been building up the rhyme
When he had better far have stretched his limbs
Beside a brook in mossy forest-dell,
By sun or moon-light, to the influxes
Of shapes and sounds and shifting elements
Surrendering his whole spirit, of his song
And of his fame forgetful! so his fame

Should share in Nature's immortality,
A venerable thing! and so his song
Should make all Nature lovelier, and itself
Be loved like Nature! But 'twill not be so;
And youths and maidens most poetical,
Who lose the deepening twilights of the spring
In ball-rooms and hot theatres, they still
Full of meek sympathy must heave their sighs
O'er Philomela's pity-pleading strains.

My Friend, and thou, our Sister! we have learnt
A different lore: we may not thus profane
Nature's sweet voices, always full of love
And joyance! 'Tis the merry Nightingale
That crowds, and hurries, and precipitates
With fast thick warble his delicious notes,
As he were fearful that an April night
Would be too short for him to utter forth
His love-chant, and disburthen his full soul
Of all its music!

        And I know a grove
Of large extent, hard by a castle huge,
Which the great lord inhabits not; and so
This grove is wild with tangling underwood,
And the trim walks are broken up, and grass,
Thin grass and king-cups grow within the paths.
But never elsewhere in one place I knew
So many nightingales; and far and near,
In wood and thicket, over the wide grove,
They answer and provoke each other's song,
With skirmish and capricious passagings,
And murmurs musical and swift jug jug,
And one low piping sound more sweet than all —
Stirring the air with such a harmony,
That should you close your eyes, you might almost
Forget it was not day!

Samuel Taylor Coleridge, April 1798

7

' . . . the merry Nightingale'

Coleridge was the first of the Romantics to reject decisively the maudlin associations of pastoral poetry and return to the optimistic, joyous bird of the medieval period. In his 'conversational poem' 'The Nightingale' he refers to the tradition (quoting Milton's words, '"Most musical, most melancholy!"' bird') only to dismiss it as the conceit of pierced self-pitying poetasters who had never truly *listened* to the bird: ' . . . some night-wandering man whose heart was pierced/ . . . And so, poor wretch! filled all things with himself,/And made all gentle sounds tell back the tale'. He suggests that the tormented poet might have done better to have gone for a tramp in the woods and surrendered himself 'to the influxes/Of shapes and sounds and shifting elements'.

This is what Coleridge himself had done. It was the spring of 1798 and he was staying with his wife Sara at Nether Stowey in the Quantocks, a couple of miles away from William and Dorothy Wordsworth's house, Alfoxden Park, near Holford. The two men were deep into their momentous collaboration on the *Lyrical Ballads*, and in the company of Dorothy (but not Sara) they often walked at night in the woods round Holford. 'The Nightingale' describes one of these expeditions in late April to a copse near Dodington Hall, just north of the Helford-Stowey road. Coleridge addresses the poem to his companions – 'My Friend, and thou our Sister' – but the 'conversation' implicitly includes the reader, too, who is led by the hand into the 'moon-lit bushes': 'Come, we will rest on this old mossy bridge!'

The date of the poem's origin is supported by a letter Coleridge wrote to Wordsworth in early May 1798, enclosing a manuscript draft of the poem. The letter consists of a marvellous snatch of doggerel which confirms Coleridge's refusal to take a solemn view of the nightingale:

> *In stale blank verse a subject stale*
> *I send per post* my *Nightingale;*
> *And like an honest bard, dear Wordsworth,*
> *You'll tell me what you think, my Bird's worth.*
> *My own opinion's briefly this —*
> *His* bill *he opens not amiss;*
> *And when he has sung a stave or so,*
> *His breast, & some small space below,*
> *So throbs & swells, that you might swear*
> *No vulgar music's working there.*
> *So far, so good; but then, 'od rot him!*
> *There's something falls off at his bottom . . .*

The whole poem is remarkably accurate in its insights into the bird's habits and natural history. Coleridge knows that it is only the male nightingale that sings, and that serenading males 'provoke' each other. He also understands the bird's habitat (the 'grove is wild with tangling underwood'), but places it, tellingly, in a derelict mansion, 'which the great lord inhabits not', making the vernacular singer displace the aristocratic owner. And as Coleridge's stanzas echo with the rhythm and rattle of the song itself, so the bird becomes (as it was to become for Keats) a symbol of freedom as well as joy:

> . . .'Tis the merry Nightingale
> That crowds, and hurries and precipitates
> With fast, thick warble his delicious notes . . .

Twenty years later, on 11 April 1819, Coleridge and Keats met on Hampstead Heath. They walked and talked for not more than three-quarters of an hour, but ranged, according to a letter by Keats, over continents of topics:

> In those two Miles he broached a thousand things – let me see if I can give you a list – Nightingales, Poetry – on Poetical Sensation – Metaphysics – Different genera and species of Dreams – Nightmare – a dream accompanied by a sense of touch – single and double touch – A dream related – First and second consciousness – the difference explained between will and Volition – so [many] metaphysicians from a want of smoking the second consciousness – Monsters – the Kraken – Mermaids – Southey believes in them – Southey's belief too much diluted – A Ghost story – Good morning – I heard his voice as he came towards me – I heard it as he moved away – I had heard it all the interval – if it may be called so.

Though Keats obviously regarded Coleridge's bombastic monologue as something of a joke, it may well have stirred in him the first thoughts of the nightingale ode. It had been a dispiriting time in his personal life. He could see no way forward in his intense love for Fanny Brawne (who was living next door at the time the ode was written). One brother, George, had emigrated to America, and the other had died of tuberculosis. John was only twenty-three but, from his medical training, had begun to suspect that he too was in the early stages of TB. His move to the clean air of Hampstead and the Vale of Health in 1817 had been partly prompted by this fear.

But the spring of 1819 seemed to offer some cheer in the gloom. The weather was perfect. Between 26 April and 18 May there was an almost unbroken run of balmy, dry days. Everything was in a state of luxuriant forwardness. Roses were in bloom on 3 May, and nightingales seemed to have returned to north London early and in some numbers. In Highgate, at least, their songs were voluminous enough to keep the dyspeptic Coleridge awake at night. (He punned about his misfortune in a letter to a friend: 'Ah! PHIlomel! Ill do thy strains accord with those of CALomel!') One bird had apparently already taken up residence in the shrubberies of Wentworth Place, where Keats was living, and he confessed to feeling 'a tranquil, continued joy' at its song.

And one fine morning, quite possibly May Day itself, he took his chair from the breakfast table into the small, secluded garden, sat under the plum tree, and wrote 'Ode to a Nightingale' in two or three hours. The Wentworth Place bird may have been singing at the time, but Keats is soon in a reverie and dreaming of more distant, poetic nightingales. He thinks of the bird's other home, and how he, too, may need to migrate to the 'warm South' for a cure; of his brother's terminal illness ('youth grows pale, and spectre-thin, and dies') and how the bird's joyous song is, and has always been, a challenge to death and decay, to 'The weariness, the fever and the fret/Here, where men sit and hear each other groan'. He wonders, not too seriously, if it might be 'rich to die/To cease upon the midnight with no pain/While thou art pouring forth thy soul abroad/In such an extasy!' But rejects the idea, almost as if it were an insult to the bird to walk out on the beauty and vitality concentrated in its song.

The musing takes him through 'faery lands', the forested landscape of 'white hawthorn and pastoral eglantine' which he had encountered in Dryden's version of the medieval nightingale poem, 'The Flower and the Leaf'. And meditating on all the generations of listeners who have been touched by the bird, he catches, just for a moment, a vision of the oneness of the world. The nightingale's song transcends him, unites singer and listener, human and nature.

But then the reverie breaks. Even if the song is immortal, the nightingale itself is not, and, a real, mobile bird again, it flies away over the heath. Keats himself is 'tolled' back to his 'sole self' – but not, I think, to such an anti-climactic state as some critics of this stanza would argue. To have caught the tension – and the resonance – between the immortal nightingale of the imagination and the flesh-and-blood bird is one of the poem's great achievements.

But it was an idea for which he was in debt to William Hazlitt. In the spring of 1818, Keats had attended Hazlitt's course of lectures on the English poets. The fifth lecture, on Thomson and Cowper, made a particular impression on him. In this, Hazlitt extends the argument that he first laid out in his famous essay 'On the Love of the Country' (1814). What distinguishes our fondness for nature from our other attachments, he suggests, is its 'abstractedness': 'The interest we feel in human nature is exclusive, and confined to the individual, the interest we feel in external nature is common, and transferable from one object to all others of the same class.' As Hazlitt extends his argument, so the inspiration for many of the images, feelings and even phrases in the nightingale ode become clear.

If we have once enjoyed the cool shade of a tree and then been lulled into a deep repose by the sound of a brook running at its foot, we are sure that wherever we can find a shady stream, we can enjoy the same pleasure again, so that when we imagine these objects, we can easily form a mystic personification of the friendly power that inhabits them, Dryad or Naiad, offering its cool fountain or its tempting shade.

Hazlitt's lecture ends with the example of familiar birds, with the nightingale itself, and with the prototype of one of the most powerful phrases in Keats's poem. 'The cuckoo,' he writes, '"that wandering voice", that comes and goes with spring, mocks our ears with one note from youth to age; and the lapwing, screaming round the traveller's path, repeats for ever the same sad story of Tereus and Philomel!'

Proud Songsters

The thrushes sing as the sun is going
  And the finches whistle in ones and pairs,
And as it gets dark loud nightingales
  In bushes
Pipe, as they can when April wears
  As if all Time were theirs.

These are brand-new birds of twelve-months growing,
Which a year ago, or less than twain,
No finches were, nor nightingales,
  Nor thrushes
But only particles of grain,
  And earth, and air, and rain.

Thomas Hardy, from *Winter Words*, 1928

8

'Provençal song, and sunburnt mirth'

Nightingales' songs can be approachable, prosaic even, as well as mesmerisingly romantic. Certainly, there are times when they make me ponder the same themes as Keats – lost youth, mortality, the continuity of nature, the hedonism of the south. But more often they seem to be singing in the spirit of Coleridge's 'merry' bird and the impish punster in 'The Owl and the Nightingale' than of that intense 'Dryad of the trees'. I have found their 'writelinge' seductive, skittish, ebullient, heartening, often funny and almost never melancholy, and over the years they have come to seem like familiars, albeit of a rather distant and elusive breed.

I often daydream about them in the winter months, working them into fantasies of escape to the sun. I imagine them as accompaniments to Provençal picnics, as cooling as fruit in the afternoon heat; and to moonlit suppers in white-stoned Andalucian villages (and then, on a more absurd flight of fancy, try to imagine the best wine for

73

drinking with the song). I think, too, of the times they have lured me out on more homely expeditions – of mild, clear nights in bluebell time in England and the sudden urge to point the car towards Suffolk. It is always a dream of heading off, of migration. I become like Rat in *The Wind in the Willows*, fretting at the onset of autumn and beguiled by the Sea Rat's tales of the Mediterranean and the swallows' 'intoxicating babble . . . of violet seas, tawny sand and lizard-haunted walls'.

Only twice have I experienced nightingales as part of my own home patch. In 1989 one sang all spring at a run-down municipal rubbish tip about a quarter of a mile from my house in the Chilterns. Its home was a steep thicket, wedged between the main Euston railway line and a battery of waste incinerators. The A41 to London was less than two hundred yards away in the other direction, and much of the time the bird was scarcely audible above the roar of trains and traffic. I first heard it at midnight one evening in mid-May, singing against an orange full moon and the glow of rubbish fires started by fly-tippers, and was lost in admiration at its magnanimity.

But I worried that it might be a solitary and unstimulated bird. There were certainly no other singing nightingales within earshot, and probably not within ten miles. I am not even sure it had a mate. Some nights I would lean out of my window and wonder if, with a lull in the traffic and a change in the wind, I might hear a snatch of the song floating into my bedroom. But I suppose that was a dream of escape, too.

In Suffolk, many years before, I had listened to them from my bedroom window. I owned a cottage in the Blyth valley for a while, and they sang the very first night I moved in. It was another hot mid-May and I had driven up to Suffolk with the car windows wound right down. All the way through the tracts of heathland that stretch from Aldeburgh to Walberswick, nightingale phrases flew, disembodied, into the car.

That night two sang close to my cottage, one in the churchyard, another in the scrubby heathland that began just fifty yards beyond the garden. I lay awake all night listening to them, puzzling about why I found their songs so poignant and evocative.

A few days later at Minsmere bird reserve on the coast, I heard an extraordinary duet between a nightingale and a nightjar. It was dusk, about an hour after sunset. The nightjar lay silhouetted along the branch of a dead oak, looking like a woody extrusion itself and turning its head slightly as it poured out its dry, reeling song. Six feet below it a nightingale sang from the deep wrappings of a blackthorn bush, in the kind of bravura performance that must have helped give rise to the old myth about the breast against the thorn. They sang together, drone and counter tenor, for nearly fifteen minutes. I had met up with a group of birders from Teesside and we stood in a silent row, gaping at this apparition of the warm south only twenty miles from Norwich. Then we all went and drank to them at the Eels Foot pub which lies on the margin between the heath and the marsh.

I was going to write that nightingales take me out of myself, transport me. But it is often just the opposite of that. They have been reassurances about fortuitous beauty and the continuity of nature and place, a kind of mascot or charm. Often I have heard them unexpectedly, on workaday business in what I thought were familiar landscapes: lining a bushy green lane at Selborne, when I was trying to trace the extent of Gilbert White's own territory; sounding from a remote wood in the New Forest, when I thought I was lost; chanting against the roar of Phantom jets flying out of Lakenheath air base in the sandy wastes of the Breckland. And on each occasion I have understood in a new way where I was.

Once I was put back in place so decisively by them that

they helped me overcome an odd and intractable phobia about 'abroad'. I had done a bit of exploring in southern Europe in my early twenties. I travelled down through Spain, swapping guitar licks with flamenco players and watching bee-eaters hawking from the telegraph wires. I spent a summer in Provence, and one dawn crept out over the Camargue salt-pans to watch the flamingo flocks close to. Then work and the responsibility of helping to nurse my mother, struck down prematurely by Parkinson's disease, stopped me venturing overseas. I soon got so out of the habit that the prospect began to fill me with dread. It wasn't a fear of flying or exotic illnesses, but of what John Clare described as 'being out of one's knowledge'. I would have nightmares of waking in a foreign house and not knowing where I was, of being unable to get home again, of having no control over what was happening to me. When I finally shook off my phobia on a winter weekend in Holland with two staunchly tolerant friends, I took with me (just in case) a handwritten card to prop up by my bed, saying DON'T PANIC – YOU ARE IN AMSTERDAM.

I put the seal on my *rites de passage* later that year with a trip to the French Pyrenees with an old rambling companion. It had been a long and claustrophobic winter in Britain, and we had mapped out a few days on the Cerdagne plateau, some 3000 feet up in reputedly the sunniest skies in France. We had fanciful hopes of drifting amongst fields of wild narcissi and drinking Catalan wine under the circling eagles. I imagined there would be nightingales too, but didn't give this familiar bird much thought beside the glamorous creatures of south-western France. I was after something new to confirm my rediscovered adventurousness.

Our drive down from Toulouse started well. There were dazzling clear skies, and packs of returning swifts rocketing through the mountain passes (bound for England, maybe!). We ignored the way patches of snow seemed to be edging ever closer to the sides of the road, and had got as far south as Ax-les-Thermes before we realised that we were driving slap back into winter. All the way through the snaking curves of the Col de Puymorens the snow was banked in high drifts by the sides of the road. There were no flowers, and the little greenery that was visible had been bent double by fresh snowfalls during the past few days. Our Pyrenean sun-trap was frozen in, and after a brief conference we aborted our arrangements and headed off south-east, towards the Mediterranean.

It seemed a disastrous decision at first. Going downhill now, the hairpins were vertiginous and exhausting. We had the wrong maps, the wrong clothes, and no clear idea of where we were heading. The temperature rose steadily, and I became increasingly disorientated by the landscape. By the time we had reached the coastal plateau, I was remembering all too fearfully the phantoms and anxieties that had trapped me in England for so long. Then the ancient clarion came to the rescue. We were passing a long cypress windbreak on the outskirts of Perpignan when, out of one of the trees, a nightingale flung a fierce, explosive phrase. In a moment, but in a way I can't properly explain, I had my bearings again. It was May, we were in the South of France, and all creatures (ourselves included) were in their proper place.

Perpignan, an effervescent Catalan town with streets smelling of dried herbs and warm laundry, proved to be a marvellous base. We spent most of our time in the maquis, the Mediterranean scrub belt of pistacia and ever-green oak, with its elaborate and motley understorey of aromatic and spiny shrubs – cistus, rosemary, lavender, box, juniper. The maquis was full of nightingales. And they seemed to be singing wherever we went, in scrub-filled roadside ditches, in overgrown farmyards, in scraggy copses of stone pine and kermes oak – anywhere there was a patch of bushy cover. They sang throughout the daylight hours in brief, intense snatches, and more flamboyantly in the evenings. But they never became mundane, just a persistent bubbling undertone to almost everything we did, like the sound of running water.

Sometimes they were more vehement. One clammy afternoon we did a tour of the little villages in the Tech valley and spent too much time inside the car. On the way back to Perpignan we stopped to stretch our legs in an abandoned quarry. It was a bizarre landscape of minute, jagged-edged vineyards and overgrown hedges. Thin wisps of smoke curled through the heat haze. There was a nightingale in almost every hedge and by the time we reached the centre of the quarry, we could hear at least a dozen singing at once. We also realised that the smoke was not blowing from some spontaneous fire in the parched scrub, but from a pile of smouldering mattresses. We were in the local rubbish tip.

But a half-memory of places like this from twenty years back, or something glimpsed unconsciously out of the corner of an eye, was nagging me, and I felt that we must go and look at a sheer quarry face about 300 yards away. I did not even need to raise my binoculars to know what the spectre was when it finally broke cover and shot vertically upwards. It was a bee-eater, as florid as an aerial exhibitionist as the nightingale is as a singer. We ran forwards and were able to get within about a hundred yards of what proved to be a group of six, lounging against each other on a tree at the top of the quarry face. And as the nightingales continued their chorus, the bee-eaters whizzed about, sometimes darting upwards after prey, sometimes gliding down, then suddenly changing direction, so that their chestnut backs shone in the sun one moment and their turquoise underparts the next.

On our last day I heard my first hoopoe. We were meandering about, listening to nightingales and admiring a meadow full of lax-flowered orchids, when I heard a sound that I thought at first had come from some kind of farm animal. To tell the truth it sounded rather like a gibbon. Then it came again, a triple-horn note, and I knew it must be a hoopoe, a bird I had never heard call before. A few seconds later I saw it fly up into a dead tree, like an immense butterfly striped in ginger and black. I raced after it – followed smartly by the farmer up whose back drive I was now jogging. He enquired – in raspy *langue d'oc*, but very courteously – whether I had any problems. I dug to the depths of my fossil French and tried to explain a chase I would have had difficulty justifying in English. But communication more ancient than national tongues came to my rescue. The hoopoe's name is onomatopoeic, and after I had pooped a few times, the farmer's eyes cleared and he said, *'Ah, l'huppe. Son nid est dans le chêne.'* In an instant, vestigial agoraphobia and a week's fuming at *chasse gardée* signs evaporated, and I relished the supreme satisfaction of making contact.

An almost ruined holiday had been well and truly rescued. So, I reckoned, had I, venturing out as a timid greenhorn and returning with a new confidence as a traveller. The nightingales and their exotic companions had a lot to do with the transformation. They seemed for those few days a kind of bridge – effervescent citizens of the south, but also reliable, comprehensible fellow-creatures.

I have heard nightingales in many parts of southern Europe since. One sang in a solitary myrtle bush in front of a Costa Brava beach development. Another year, they staked out their pitches like buskers in the small north Majorcan village where I was staying with friends in April. One lived in the lemon grove behind the house; he serenaded us as we sipped drinks on the balcony at sunset and watched the black vultures circling to roost above the crags. Another sang much later in the night, from the depths of a garden that we toiled past on our way back from the restaurant.

My favourites haunt the tangled edges of the River Dourbie in the limestone country west of the Cévennes.

This has become my favourite piece of France, an almost annual retreat, and for me its nightingales have acquired a rather laid-back urbanity, like young cronies from the local bars. One late May night, under a full moon and a sky lacy with stars, three riverside birds with territories about a hundred yards apart sang at midnight, in strict order, for just five minutes each. In this place of highly local character (Auden called the southern limestone 'this region of short distances and definite places'), singing in one's own spot at one's own special moment is enough to establish identity.

The one thing nightingales never became for me were the Cupids beloved of medieval troubadours and modern songwriters. But for the time Lily and I were together, nightingales – and for that matter all kinds of other birds – insisted on being part of the relationship. She lived in a cottage in Surrey, the nightingale's one-time heartland, the site of Tennyson's and Gerard Manley Hopkins's poems and Beatrice Harrison's celebrated cello duet. Lily had heard one in the garden the spring before we met, and in spring there were always chiffchaffs and blackcaps singing yards from her window. (She also kept geese, which she insisted on calling 'gooses'. It was a piece of affectionate whimsy that still makes my throat catch and which so touched me with its note of respect that I have tried to remember since that nightingales, too, are individuals, and not members of that abstract collective '*the* nightingale'.)

With that heightened perception that sometimes accompanies romantic affairs, I soon rediscovered a slight gift for intuiting and predicting where we might see unusual birds. I succeeded in conjuring up a great grey shrike on Frensham Common and a short-eared owl on exactly the same north Norfolk marsh where I had watched one twenty years before. Wherever we went we saw woodpeckers, usually in pairs, and they became a tongue-in-cheek private symbol for us, and a way of imagining what the other was doing or thinking when we were apart. ('One was carrying a stick' Lily said hopefully after a pair flew past early one spring.)

She was playing a sophisticated vamp in a TV comedy series at the time, and when she was interviewed by a listings magazine about her own most romantic dream, she replied 'listening to nightingales with someone you are fond of, and not having to talk'. I don't believe that either she or the magazine knew of the anciently ribald meaning of the phrase. But I did, and liked to think it was beamed specifically at me.

Anyway, the idea of genuinely listening to nightingales together turned from a whim into a serious yearning; and failing totally to find any in Surrey that year, we planned a trip to the South of France, starting in Lily's favourite Dordogne and moving down to the Languedoc.

I didn't know what to expect from the Dordogne, which is so often mocked for having become a kind of pastoral theme park for the English. But it reminded me of an immense southerly version of the English chalk downs. The Dordogne river itself is hundreds of yards wide during its passage through the limestone, and is edged by shallows and bays and wild willow thickets. On our first evening we sat side by side on the bank in a haze of sound. Fish were jumping, crickets scratching and behind us, from a poplar grove, came the liquid, musing warbles of golden orioles. We heard our first nightingales together as we were walking back to the hotel. They were bustling about in riverside scrub by wooden bridge, and active enough to be visible. I was far too excited to have the gumption *not* to talk.

Thereafter the perfectly romantic nightingale, communed over in silence, eluded us. Roadside birds sang in such extravagant ensembles that they demanded not just talk but programme notes. Hotel birds were usually too

distant. In Domme there were several singing outside our
bedroom window, but first Lily was detained in the bath-
room as a consequence of a surfeit of *eau de noix*, then I
lost my hearing aid. By the time we were both composed
the birds had stopped singing.

It didn't really matter. By the river, or in the hilltop
villages on the ridge, bird song and sun seemed to melt
preset resolutions and soften boundaries. Whenever we
sat outside a café, there was always a black redstart darting
about from window-ledge to rooftop above us, its terse,
metallic song ringing down the street. Near the River Lot,
we heard a wryneck chiming *inside* a hollow walnut tree.
And, just as there had been when I was in southern France
years before, there were nightingales everywhere, whatever the conditions. We even heard them singing – or at
least whistling brief, consoling phrases to themselves –
3000 feet up in the cool, mist-wreathed heights of the
Corbières hills, in scrub thick with sodden orchids.

By the time we reached the edge of the Mediterranean
zone the weather had begun to turn. We decided to put
up for one night in an auberge in the spa village of Alet-
les-Bains, on the banks of the River Aude. It was a gloomy
hotel in what seemed to me a soporific town, and as the
atmosphere turned more humid and oppressive, I had, to
Lily's understandable bemusement, a return of my old
twinges of disorientation and anxiety. Nowhere seems
more entrapping than a small town under a flat grey sky.

But the hotel, set at the edge of a derelict medieval
abbey, had its own healing powers. That evening, we sat
outside, drank black wine (Ricardelle de la Clape!) and
filled ourselves with cassoulet. The cloud passed, the hotel
garden filled up with garrulous tourists and Alet-les-Bains
began to seem a very agreeable place. At dusk the owls
started, the heavy boom of eagle owls in the distance and
a cacophony of tawnies in trees all around the hotel. We
stole out through the garden, and by the walls of the
ruined abbey saw them flickering through the hotel lamp-

light, followed by a stream of bats. At our feet the glow-worms were coming alight, and we felt enchanted.

Our room, too, seemed a relic of the Middle Ages, with a bed as bowed as a glaciated valley and a sit-up tub for a bath. We laughed ourselves to sleep, while outside the nightingales did their best to serenade us, but were drowned out by the roar of the river. They were hardly the rhapsodical birds of Bernard de Ventadour, but for my money were cheerier and more festive company.

from
The Nightingale's Nest

Up this green woodland ride lets softly rove
& list the nightingale – she dwelleth here
Hush let the wood gate softly clap – for fear
The noise might drive her from her home of love
For here Ive heard her many a merry year
At morn & eve nay all the live long day
As though she lived on song – this very spot
Just where the old mans beard all wildly trails
Rude arbours oer the rode & stops the way
& where that child its blue bell flowers hath got
Laughing & creeping through the mossy rails
There have I hunted like a very boy
Creeping on hands & knees through matted thorns
To find her nest & see her feed her young
& vainly did I many hours employ
All seemed as hidden as a thought unborn
& where these crimping fern leaves ramp among
The hazels underboughs – Ive nestled down
& watched her while she sung – & her renown
Hath made me marvel that so famed a bird
Should have no better dress then russet brown
Her wings would tremble in her extacy
& feathers stand on end as 'twere with joy
& mouth wide open to release her heart
Of its out sobbing songs – the happiest part
Of summers fame she shared . . .

   Sing on sweet bird may no worse hap befall
Thy visions then the fear that now decieves
We will not plunder music of its dower
Nor turn this spot of happiness to thrall
For melody seems hid in every flower

That blossoms near thy home – these harebells all
Seems bowing with the beautiful in song
& gaping cuckoo with its spotted leaves
Seems blushing of the singing it has heard
How curious is the nest no other bird
Uses such loose materials or weaves
Their dwellings in such spots – dead oaken leaves
Are placed without & velvet moss within
& little scraps of grass – & scant & spare
Of what seems scarce materials down & hair
For from mans haunts she seemeth naught to win
Yet nature is the builder & contrives
Homes for her childrens comfort even here
Where solitudes deciples spend their lives
Unseen save when a wanderer passes near
That loves such pleasant places – Deep adown
The nest is made an hermits mossy cell
Snug lies her curious eggs in number five
Of deadened green or rather olive brown
& the old prickly thorn bush guards them well
& here we'll leave them still unknown to wrong
As the old woodlands legacy of song

John Clare, c. 1832, from *The Midsummer Cushion*, first
published 1978

9

'Hidden as a thought unborn'

Both the public history and the personal experience of
nightingales seems inexorably qualified with associations
and metaphors. Yet sometimes this compulsive desire to
find meanings in the song can seem like taking liberties
with the bird. The nightingale is a creature in its own right,
not just a symbol or a source of happenstance background
music. Even Gilbert White, a deeply sympathetic lover of
birds, distanced himself from presumptuous claims about
– and to – the bird's song. In 1789, just ten years before
the publication of the *Lyrical Ballads* (which marked the
formal beginning of the Romantic movement, and
included Coleridge's 'conversation poem' on the nightingale), he wrote that 'the language of birds is very
ancient, and, like other ancient modes of speech, very
elliptical: little is said, but much is meant and understood.'
But White meant understood by other birds, not us. Whatever is going on when we listen in to nightingales, it
certainly isn't a dialogue.

The poet Kim Taplin came up against this conundrum

– the recognition that she was being touched by a voice that made no rational sense to her – one summer in Oxfordshire. She was walking along the River Cherwell close to her home, amongst the bankside tangle of alder and nettle and meadowsweet. It was a humid afternoon, and, hot and stung, she retreated to the shade, and 'obliged to give up trying to possess the secrets of the place and sit quietly, they had a chance to take possession of me'.

Then she heard – without any intention or preconceptions – a bird singing from the undergrowth. It wasn't a nightingale and probably not the local rarity, a marsh warbler. In fact she was not sure what kind of bird it was. That was what struck her so powerfully about the song. It was not full of specific warbler codes or elaborate symbols, but seemed to be pared down to that most fundamental of natural signals: 'fellow creature here':

> Its song . . . was full of delight but it did not have
> me rapt, nor was it wistful or cheerful or any of the
> anthropomorphic adjectives we use in trying to
> 'capture' birds' song in words. And I have no view
> on whether it sang 'I love you' or 'Keep off' to some
> invisible mate or rival. I only knew that it seemed
> to sing itself, as it was itself, without self-
> consciousness, and that I felt immeasurably lucky to
> be there.

She instinctively felt, too, that it seemed to live there by a more certain right than her own.

I understand her feelings. Yet I have never been able to feel entirely excluded from a nightingale's performance, or from its habitat. When I listen to a bird, any bird, singing, I don't feel like a intruder or voyeur (as I do sometimes when, say, watching feeding or mating). I know that, strictly speaking, I am, that the singing is neither for my benefit nor even for the benefit of most other birds, but is scored for and directed at neighbours

of the same species. But it still seems too public, too indiscriminately thrown into the air, too capable of arousing
human emotions to be neatly compartmented off like that.
Rightly or wrongly, I feel *included*.

When I first began pursuing nightingales, I was struck
by how often they seemed to choose some kind of natural
amphitheatre to perform from. In my first spring in Suffolk
– that hot May full of nightingales – I heard birds in all
kinds of arenas. Perched one early morning on the edge
of a sunken tennis court on Aldeburgh common (approxi-
mately where the umpire might sit), I listened while a bird
served short, piercing phrases from dense scrub behind
the base-line, filling the glade of shorn grass and straight
white lines with an incongruously wild skirling. A few
miles to the north I came across the remains of a Second
World War gun-emplacement, half swallowed up by steep
barrows of blackthorn, broom and gorse. Its concrete base
was already too hot to sit on in the late morning sun, but
that diminutive hollow, smelling of peach and coconut
from the broom flowers, was the focus of another nightingale's fitful but tireless noon-time song. Later I heard
another car-park bird, in a thorn clump shading the
entrance to Newdelights Walk in the Walberswick heath-
lands.

What is going on here? Do the birds have a taste for
spaces which add sonorousness to their song? Is there
anything in the old belief that they favour sites where
there is an echo? Or is it simply a matter of my choosing
a miniature arena to listen in, of seeking a hideaway in
the bushes in much the same way as the bird itself? I have
made burrows like this, places to lie up, ever since I was
a child, and maybe this has helped make me instinctively
sympathetic towards the bird.

The secretiveness of nightingales can make them seem
like outlaw birds, creatures of the maquis, singing against
the world. It is an association which has been emphasised

by their reputation for singing during trench fighting and bombing raids – cocking a snook at the war, or playing the heroic bugler, depending on who is relating the story. They probably do not sing more than other species in these conditions (many birds are provoked by loud noise), but they are remarked on more, especially for the apparently poignant irony of exquisite song co-existing with the chaos of battle.

I heard nightingales once on the Ministry of Defence's tank-training ranges in Dorset, just a few days after the Chernobyl nuclear reactor had blown up in 1986. It had been the worst of all possible springs. At the beginning of May, three days after the explosion, the hedgerows were still silent and shrivelled, and the sky the colour of church-roof lead. Then a pressure front loaded with radioactive isotopes had sent numbing winds across most of Europe. It did not seem to deter the nightingales. Tramping the Tyneham ranges during the second weekend in May, I heard their songs floating up against the gales. They were singing, it seemed, from *under* the ground, from old shell craters that now brimmed with dense blackthorn scrub. In the charged atmosphere of that day their songs seemed wildly ambivalent – pathetic, indomitable, indifferent; swan-songs of defiance. But they, of course, knew nothing of this and were, as Kim Taplin wrote, just singing for themselves.

It was the Northamptonshire poet John Clare who most closely located the common ground between ourselves and the bird in his poem 'The Nightingale's Nest'. It was a work which summed up his lifelong hostility to the over-weening appropriation of nature. In the winter of 1824 he had written to his publishers Taylor and Hessey stating unequivocally what he thought about current urban attitudes to nightingales:

I forgot to say in my last that the Nightingale sung
as common by day as night & as often tho its a fact
that it is not generaly known your Londoners are
very fond of talking about this bird & I believe fancy
every bird they hear after sunset a Nightingale I
remember when I was there last while walking with
a friend in the fields of Shacklwell we saw a
gentleman & lady listning very attentive by the side
of a shrubbery and when we came up we heard them
lavishing praises on the beautiful song of the
nightingale which happend to be a thrush but it did
for them & they listend & repeated their praise with
heart felt satisfaction while the bird seemed to know
the grand distinction that its song had gaind for it
& strive exultingly to keep up the deception by
attempting a varied & more louder song the dews
was ready to fall but the lady was heedless of the
wet grass . . . such is the ignorance of nature in
large Citys that are nothing less than over grown
prisons that shut out the world & all its beautys.

Clare may well have numbered his publishers among such
gushing amateurs. But he quite probably had Keats in
mind, too. In a letter written nine years after Keats's death,
he criticises the poet for describing 'nature as she . . .
appeared in his fancys & not as he would have described
her if he had witnessed the things he describes'. To Clare
the essence of poetry was faithfulness to both the
observed, material world and to the imagination, the
'poetic eye'. He was, as the critic Hugh Haughton has
pointed out, above all the poet of *seeing*.

Clare knew nightingales as fellow creatures of the copse
long before he knew their status as poetic symbols and as
what he called 'the popular voice of music'. When he was
a boy he loved to listen to their 'restless song' as he passed
their 'black thorn bower', and knew them from several
sites in his home village of Helpston, on the edge of the
Cambridgeshire fens. Every year nightingales nested in

Royce Wood, close to the village, and Clare's journals and notes are full of observations about the bird. He describes its skulking habits whilst feeding in the undergrowth and its great reluctance to fly in the open. He mentions that he has never once found a nest without oak leaves. He notes a thrush which learned phrases from a nightingale, and gives a vivid account of the quiet song sometimes heard in the proximity of the nest:

> she whistled without effort – never raising the
> feathers of her throat & neck & head as I had seen
> her but piping as quietly as the Robin & as if the
> song came almost involuntary without her knowing
> it.

And after his observation (made in May 1832, when he was living at Northborough, three miles from Helpston), he confesses that he is wrong to have called nightingales 'she' and that he is '*almost* certain that the female is silent & never sings'. In the same year he makes the best attempt that exists in nineteenth-century literature to transcribe the notes of the song, from a bird singing in the orchard outside his window:

> Chee chew chee chew chee
> chew – cheer cheer cheer
> chew chew chew chee
> – up cheer up cheer up
> tweet tweet tweet jug jug jug
>
> wew wew wew – chur chur
> woo it woo it tweet tweet
> tweet jug jug jug
>
> tee rew tee rew tee rew – gur
> gur – chew rit chew rit – chur-chur-chur
> chur will-will will-will tweet-em
> tweet em jug jug jug jug

grig grig grig chew chew

wevy wit wevy wit
wevy wit – cheet-chit
chee-chit chee chit
weewit weewit wee
wit cheer cheer
cheer – pelew
pelew pelew —
bring a jug bring a
jug bring a jug

All this experience is worked into 'The Nightingale's Nest'.
The poem begins in much the same way as Coleridge's
tribute. The reader is taken by the hand and led into the
poem by the device of being led into the thicket (Royce
Wood) itself: 'Up this green woodland ride lets softly rove/
& list the nightingale . . .' Yet though Clare shares Coleridge's view of the song – 'its luscious strain . . . the happiest part/Of summers fame she shared' – he does not
listen to it at a distance, as a member of an audience. Clare
knows this wood as well as the bird does; he *shares* its
territory:

& where these crimping fern leaves ramp among
The hazels underboughs – Ive nestled down
& watched her while she sung . . .

Unlike Keats's nightingale, which was fabulous, immortal,
abstract, Clare's is a particular bird, placed in an exact spot
inside the territory of the parish ('Aye as I live her secret
nest is here/Up on this white thorn stulp'). Clare isn't
glibly identifying with the bird, but he does see it as a
fellow commoner, making a livelihood on the marginal
lands, even wearing similar garb:

. . . her renown
Hath made me marvel that so famed a bird
Should have no better dress than russet brown.

It is too, a fellow artist, a maker not just of music but of
an exquisite, unpretentious nest – 'an hermits mossy cell',
whose construction he spells out in affectionate detail. But
Clare goes to some length to differentiate himself from the
bird, and would, I think, have agreed with John Berger's
words: 'Art does not imitate nature, it imitates creation.'
He is meticulous in celebrating the nightingale as an individual, something exterior to himself. He understands its
fears and, respecting its privacy, finally leaves it 'still
unknown to wrong/As the old woodlands legacy of song'.
The song is both his and the bird's. The old woodland is
both Royce Wood and all of England's ancient forest, a
once common heritage which he had seen being whittled
away by enclosure and appropriation in his own lifetime.
If 'The Nightingale's Nest' celebrates the individuality of
both poet and bird, it also warns about their shared vulner-
ability.

The old woodland's legacy has continued to be looted.
The landscape which Clare said 'made my being', on the
edge of the Cambridgeshire fens, has been enclosed,
drained, uprooted, clipped, ploughed and added to the
indistinguishable arable wastes that now stretch from
Lincolnshire to central Suffolk. When I last walked
through it was hard to believe that I was in the same
country Clare wrote about. Royce (now Rice) Wood has
become a manicured forestry plantation. The hollow lanes
have been straightened or stopped up. His 'pleasant
places' – Langley Bush and Puddocks Nook and Hilly
Snow, his blackthorn clumps and pulpit oaks – have been
levelled and obliterated. I was there in mid-May, nightingale time, but in most of Clare's old spots there was not
even the possibility of a nightingale.

Only on the remains of Emmonsales (or Ailsworth
Heath, now Castor Hanglands National Nature Reserve)
have the birds clung on. This is three miles south of Help-

ston and was at the very edge of Clare's confined and frugal world. He had strayed there when he was very young and had 'rambled among the furze the whole day till I got out of my knowledge when the very wild flowers and birds seemd to forget me and I imagined they were the inhabitants of new countrys . . .'

On that mid-May morning, with grim aptness, the heath hung under a dank mist. At noon my breath was still coming out in wintry clouds, and the cowslips and cuckoo flowers underfoot were bent under the weight of water. I heard the first nightingale about 200 yards away, its song muffled by the fog to a ratchety staccato. It was warming up more than singing, firing off short, disjointed phrases and clipped end-notes, like semi-colons. Another joined in about thirty yards away, in blackthorn scrub which had been heavily grazed by sheep and deer. I heard just one more that day, at the other end of the reserve, which seemed a sad total for what had once been the best local site for the bird.

Later I learned that nightingales had been declining on the reserve since a high point in the early 1980s. Wherever I went that summer the story was the same. At Kingley Vale, the great horseshoe of yew wood and chalk scrub that opens out on to Chichester harbour, there was not a single bird. In the late 1960s this had the highest density of birds ever formally recorded in England (13.8 pairs per square kilometre). Since then, the warden, Richard Williamson, told me, they have dwindled away, two pairs only between 1985 and '90 and then none at all.

The decline round Selborne has followed almost the same pattern. Since 1962 Stephen Povey has regularly cycled along the lanes that join Oakhanger and Worldham, just north of the village. They are lined with deep, sometimes double, hedges and tracts of old coppice woodland. On a May evening in 1962 he counted twenty-three singing nightingales along the three-mile route. By 1974 the number had dropped to eleven (I heard four in a single stretch of this road in 1981), and by 1985 to three. Since 1987 there have been no birds along this route, nor anywhere else in the entire parish. Throughout England the nightingale has now retreated south-eastwards and is only present in any number in Suffolk, Essex and Kent. Yet even the extreme south-east can no longer offer anything like the experience of the Kent survey in 1970. In a long vigil between midnight and dawn on 24 May, 167 observers heard – and with remarkable composure, logged – 977 separate nightingales. The national population has plummeted from tens of thousands of pairs in the 1950s to probably no more than 2000 pairs in the 1990s.

The causes of the crash are complex, almost certainly involving climate change, the end of coppice management in some places and the grazing away of dense ground-level scrub in others. But their consequence in Britain has been to make the nightingale even more a creature of rumour and mythology, and less the real-life bird-of-a-feather celebrated by John Clare.

from
A Nightingale Sang in Berkeley Square

That certain night, the night we met,
there was magic abroad in the air.
There were angels dining at the Ritz,
And a nightingale sang in Berkeley Square.

The moon that lingered over London Town,
poor puzzled moon, he wore a frown,
How could he know we two were so in love,
The whole darn' world seemed upside down,

The streets of Town were paved with stars,
it was such a romantic affair,
And as we kiss'd and said 'goodnight'
A nightingale sang in Berkeley Square.

When dawn came stealing up, all gold and blue,
to interrupt our rendezvous,
I still remember how you smiled and said,
'Was that a dream, or was it true?'

Eric Maschwitz and Manning Sherwin
© 1940, Reproduced by permission of
Peter Maurice Music Co Ltd

10

'Magic abroad in the air'

Even between the wars, the nightingale must have seemed like a bird from mythology for most people in Britain – not so much because its slow decline may already have started, but because the human population now largely lived where nightingales did not, or could not, live. Although they can be accommodating parish birds in Britain, they have never haunted urban areas in the way they sometimes do in southern Europe.

It was to try and bring the song to city dwellers that Beatrice Harrison hatched her famous plan to broadcast the bird's song live from her garden in Surrey. She was, in the 1920s, the most distinguished British cellist by a long margin. Delius dedicated his Cello Sonata to her. She was Elgar's favourite soloist and he chose her to make the first recording of his Cello Concerto. In 1922, when she was thirty, she moved with her family to Foyle Riding, an isolated house set in woodland south of Oxted. The following spring the weather was fine enough to tempt her into practising in the garden, sitting on a rustic seat

99

set in a sea of bluebells. One afternoon she was in the middle of Rimsky-Korsakov's 'Chant Hindou' when a bird began to sing along with her. She was understandably astonished and began to trill up and down the scales. The bird, she reported, followed her notes 'in thirds, and always perfectly in tune with the cello'. The gardener identified the bird as a nightingale and congratulated Beatrice on bringing it back to Foyle Riding, after years of absence.

In the spring of 1924 she made her broadcasting debut, in a performance of Elgar's Cello Concerto (conducted by the composer) at the Central Hall, Westminster. Halfway through, touched by the thought of the many thousands of listeners she was playing to, she hatched the idea of broadcasting the nightingales singing in her wood. She was determined to present the plan to Lord Reith, Director General of the BBC, himself, but had a long tussle persuading him to support it. Reith argued, in what were already familiar terms, that the cost would be prohibitive, the birds too unpredictable, and that he would be accused of killing conversation and encouraging secondhand experiences. What would happen, he protested, if people preferred listening to the nightingale singing from the loudspeaker rather than from the woods and lanes? (He referred to the 'tinned nightingale', perhaps recalling the Hans Christian Andersen story.) Beatrice, for her part, pleaded the cause of all those who had no access to woods and lanes, let alone real nightingales, in their daily lives, arguing that the song could not fail to uplift them.

Her trump card was the fact that the birds would now burst into song whenever she played her cello in the woods. Lord Reith, élitist and puritan though he was, was also a broadcaster and realised that he could create something of a coup – the very first live outdoor broadcast – at the same time as salving his conscience. Art coaxing nature into a euphonious duet was altogether different from a piece of ornithological vox pop. Reith gave the scheme his personal support. There was a trial, which went well, and the broadcast was scheduled for the evening of Saturday 19 May.

Two van-loads of equipment and a large battalion of engineers arrived at Foyle Riding that day and set up the operation in the garden. The microphone was placed as close as possible to the bird's usual singing post, and the amplifiers were stacked in the summerhouse. The broadcast had been announced in advance, with much trumpeting in the press. The plan was to wait until the bird was in full song and then break into the Savoy Orpheans' Saturday night dance programme.

Beatrice put on her best concert frock and went out into the garden to play for what was likely to be the biggest audience of her life. It was a clear, warm night with a full moon. So that the microphone could pick up both the bird and her cello, she had been positioned in a ditch close to the bush in which the bird usually performed.

> I placed my chair half in and half out of it, quite
> crooked, but I knew the exquisite voice was there,
> under a thicket of oak leaves, ready to sing to his
> little wife.

But he proved to be a very shy serenader. Beatrice tried playing 'Danny Boy', parts of the Elgar concerto and snatches of Dvorak, all to no avail. Donkeys brayed, engineers tripped over in the dark, rabbits gnawed the vital cable, but no nightingale sang.

Then, just after 10.45, twenty minutes before the station was due to go off the air, the bird began. An excited continuity announcer broke into the Orpheans, and for the next fifteen minutes the BBC's audience listened entranced to the historic duet. And 'duet' isn't a fanciful description of the performance. Although the bird doesn't literally follow or copy the music, there is no doubt that it is responding to the phrases coming from Beatrice's cello, like a loosely improvised cadenza over a bass ground.

The broadcast was a sensation. A million people listened in, and the programme was picked up as far afield as Italy, Paris, Barcelona and Hungary – and in areas such as Scandinavia and Scotland where real nightingales had never been heard. Many listened on crystal sets, and those who did not have their own receivers enlisted friends to relay the broadcast to them over the telephone. In some places where the radio (or its loudspeaker) was out of doors, listeners reported the broadcast spurring other real nightingales into song. Over the months that followed Beatrice Harrison received 50,000 letters of appreciation. It was almost as if the act of broadcasting, putting the nightingale one stage further removed from the listeners, had heightened its already secretive appeal.

Beatrice Harrison proved to be a great champion of the birds. On a tour of America with a programme of performances and talks, she regularly gave out her home address to audiences, inviting them to visit Foyle Riding and hear nightingales for themselves – an invitation which many hundreds took up. On 13 May 1933 she held a Nightingale Festival at the house, to raise money and support for the Royal Society for the Protection of Birds, and especially for Lord Buckmaster's bill to outlaw the catching and selling of skylarks. Foyle Riding was open from 4 p.m. till dawn the following morning. The magazine *Bird Notes and News* ran a report on the day:

> The nightingales happily did not disappoint
> listeners, for when they sank into silence and
> possibly disapproved of the lights of a mile of motor
> cars that flowed over the car parks, the chinks of
> plates and many voices, Miss Harrison wandered
> down with her magic instrument and lured them to
> song again.

The 'Cello and Nightingale' experiment was repeated with

great success in June 1924, and then made an annual event. On one occasion it was staged in a damp part of the wood, the cello set off a chorus of frogs, which was faithfully broadcast as part of the ensemble performance. It continued for twelve years, until Beatrice Harrison moved house, and was then carried on sporadically, featuring the nightingales by themselves, until 1942.

The nineteenth of May that year should have been, to the day, the eighteenth anniversary of the first broadcast. What happened instead has been recorded for the BBC archives by Sam Bonner, duty engineer for the evening. The operation got under way as usual, with tantalising uncertainty. The birds were fitful, the broadcasters on edge. But after two or three false starts, Sam Bonner felt they were singing well enough for him to authorise the break into the late-night dance-music programme. Then, through his headphones, he became aware of the distant hum of approaching aircraft. It was, we know now, the beginning of the 'Thousand Bomber' raid on Mannheim. Bonner knew nothing of the details, but realised that this was not the kind of noise to broadcast live during the middle of a war and made an urgent call to his London producer, Franklin Englemann, to shut down the transmission channel. Fortunately he was also aware that what was happening was a unique and historic piece of actuality, and asked for access to a recording channel. One was rapidly made available and, as a result, there still exists a long and unsettling record of this duet between a single nightingale and a fleet of bombers, as extraordinary in its own way as the performances with the cello. The throb of the aircraft swells remorselessly for nearly four minutes before ebbing slowly away for another three, and for the whole duration of the record the nightingale sings unwaveringly. Over that painfully stretched time its song becomes an indomitable warning note round which you cannot escape meditating upon the different faces of war.

Eric Maschwitz and Manning Sherwin's song 'A Nightingale Sang in Berkeley Square', quoted at the beginning of this chapter, is, by contrast, unashamedly escapist. Yet it too is about the paradox of song in the midst of strife. It was written in 1940, at the height of the Blitz, and is as much an evocative picture of London at war as a story of enraptured lovers. The city is under black-out, bathed in moonlight as it has not been for centuries, so that its streets are 'paved with stars'. A nightingale seems to sing from the silhouetted trees in the square, and the starstruck lovers forget 'the weariness, the fever and the fret' and imagine instead Keats's bird singing just for them: 'I still remember how you smiled and said, "Was that a dream, or was it true?" ' Much the same kind of hopeful images were being attached to the nightingale in times of trouble and sadness nearly a millennium before.

Just as nightingales occasionally imitate human music, so, for centuries, composers have tried to capture or copy the bird's song. There is even a small whistle-like instrument called the nightingale which was used to mimic the bird by Scarlatti in his Oratorio, and by Haydn and Romberg in their 'Toy' symphonies. (The lower part of the whistle is held in a glass of water which produces a clear, bubbling tone, a little like some of the bird's simpler phrases. In Hans Christian Andersen's story 'The Nightingale', the Chinese court ladies, smitten by the 'lovable coquetterie' of the song, achieved the same effect by putting water in their mouths, 'so as to gurgle when anyone spoke to them'.) Schubert, Gounod, Saint-Saëns, Tchaikovsky, Rimsky-Korsakov and Handel especially, all wrote pieces inspired by or echoing the song. Respighi actually incorporated part of an early phonograph recording of the bird into performances of his orchestral piece *The Pines of Rome*.

The most lyrically evocative – though of a very reflective

and languorous bird – is probably Granados's 'Quejas, o la maja y el ruiseñor' (Lament, or Beauty and the Nightingale) from his piano suite *Goyescas* (1911); and the most naturalistic, the duet between the woodlark and nightingale in Olivier Messiaen's *Catalogue d'Oiseaux* (1956–58). Messiaen was fascinated by bird songs from an early age, and was gifted with an ear acute enough for him to transcribe them in the wild. The songs, of course, couldn't be accurately reproduced inside the restrictions of conventional notation; birds sing in freer rhythms and at pitches which only occasionally correspond to Western chromatic scales. But what Messiaen was able to write down was sufficiently 'true' to act as a catalyst for his own composition. (Like John Clare he saw analogies between the *acts* of singing and composition.) In the *Catalogue d'Oiseaux* he combines these reworkings of the rhythm and essential structure of the song with an atmospheric, tonal picture of the natural habitat in which the performance is taking place. These are his own evocative notes of the woodlark/nightingale duet:

> From the col of the Grand Bois at St-Sauveur en Rue, in the mountains of the Forez. Pinewoods to the right of the road, meadows to the left. High in the sky, in the darkness, the Woodlark peel off two-by-two: a chromatic, fluid descent. Hidden in a thicket, in a clearing in the wood, a Nightingale responds, its biting tremolos set in contrast with the mysterious voice on high. A Woodlark, invisible, draws near, fades. The trees and fields are dark and still. It is midnight.

The problems of reflecting the nightingale's song in music go beyond the obvious limitations imposed by musical conventions. They are complicated by the difficulty – and impertinence – of trying to represent one genus of music in the style of another, of attempting, say, to play Stravinsky in the manner of Bach. The songs of birds have their own musical integrity. It would be hard to make more compact or complete musical compositions than the single phrases of a nightingale's song. They have structure, a central motif and a whole range of organised musical effects – glissandi, percussive notes, harmonics, changes in volume and tone.

But the full extent of these only becomes apparent when we listen to the song in, as it were, birds' time. Birds' sense of hearing is much more acute and discriminating than ours, and their songs compress musical information at pitches and speeds which are beyond the scope of human ears. (Some single nightingale notes, for instance, are only 1/149 seconds long.) The only way these details can be brought into our perception is to slow the songs down to a quarter or even an eighth of their 'natural' speed.

The composer David Hindley has been experimenting with this technique since the 1960s and extending it to meticulous computer-assisted analysis and musical notation of the songs. He has analysed the songs of the woodlark and skylark (200 notes a second in some trills) and reconstructed them inside musical compositions. He has also been able to transcribe the nightingale's song from recordings (he has never heard a 'live' one). At quarter speed the song is barely recognisable. It becomes an awesome recital of modernist effects – slides, whoops, percussive trills. Most remarkably, what seem like single notes at natural speed resolve at slow speeds into sonorous, velvet chords of up to four discrete notes (birds' larynxes are able to produce several notes simultaneously). It is like the orchestrated noise of a whole tropical forest and, to human ears, has little of the pleasant, accessible musicality of the song at normal speed. Yet for David Hindley it echoes the expressionism of early Webern, and he detects in it many formal music devices, most of them opposites of one kind or another, regularly and directly juxtaposed – loud and soft, high and low, short and long, single note and chord. Sliding notes are characteristic, as is the frequent occurrence of fourths and fifths, the 'perfect' intervals. There is little, too, that is strictly *un*musical: e.g. ugly inversions, ebbs and flows in inappropriate order.

As with many birds, the nightingale's song appears to have a formal musical structure at its heart that matches the informal musicality perceived at 'natural' speed by the human ear. Birds even seem to 'enjoy' their songs in the same way as humans. The songs of juvenile birds, for instance, aren't utilitarian territorial advertisements, but are soft, free-flowing, playful. This 'immature', improvisatory style (to which adults sometimes revert) may have a rough structure which is innate and unique to each species, but this does not mean that it is entirely automatic. It is spontaneous and inventive and seems to have much in common with the play of young mammals.

There are also increasing numbers of reports of birds playing at sound-making by moving or dropping objects, repeating the action over and over again, and giving signs of listening for the sound effect it produces, as a kind of 'reward'.

Even when birds are singing territorially in the breeding season, their songs are far from crudely functional. The distinguished ornithologist Charles Hartshorne wrote in 1958:

> There is without doubt a good deal of utility. But it is not the narrowly bound immediate utility of growl, whine or alarm-note; its results are not usually to be brought about the next moment, but only in the course of hours or days (a long time for a bird); they are not limited to a single outcome, but to several very different ones (securing a mate, warning rivals off territory, maintaining the pair bond).
>
> Since there is not an immediate and single practical meaning for song, it will not have a crude or narrowly emotional character, like sheer hostility as

in growls, or sheer misery as in some piteous howlings, but will be such as to fit a more balanced and normally cheerful, though mildly excited state, such as is suitable both to interest in a mate and to interest in the privacy of territory. Be it noted that maintaining a territory – and still more, attracting a mate – is only intermittently a desperate, all-or-none affair like keeping possession of a meat-bone. It is, much of the time, leisurely and pleasant; there is seldom an extreme emergency, when anything terrible can happen quickly. It is not to be imagined that a bird engaged in territorial singing for hours is exclusively reacting to the possibility of a successful invasion. There is ample room, and some probable need, for its activity to be sustained by the interest of the activity itself, both as a muscular exercise and as the production of a pattern of sound which the bird itself is well aware of.

There are so many ways in which bird song seems to be a precursor of music that it might be more appropriate to describe music as 'bird song-like' than bird song as musical. The American naturalist David Raines Wallace has suggested that our brains may retain, at the deepest level, the structures and mental charts of our reptilian and bird-like ancestors:

> I suppose this is why so many people feel a sense of affinity with birds. Our admiration for their bright colours, sweet songs, and graceful flight suggests that some very large part of our brains is still up in the canopy with them . . .

Certainty primitive human music, like bird song, shows playfulness, utility and direct expression of feelings. A good deal of folk song even shares the precise musical characteristics of nightingale song – gapped scales, common occurrence of perfect intervals, improvisation within a set structure, frequent pauses. Cecil Sharp, on his

Appalachian folk song collecting expeditions, also noted echoes of a kind of territoriality in vernacular music, with particular songs associated with particular places and times in the daily life of the community. One singer, unable to recall a song, said, 'If only I were driving the cart home I could sing it at once.' Perhaps all art is rooted – at least in part – in territorial and courtship display.

But I have to say that, for me, the experience of listening to nightingales has never felt like a close encounter with my cultural forebears. I can see the evolutionary and structural steps that might lead from song to music, but my feelings refuse to follow them. I have no instinct for appropriating or subsuming or even identifying with the bird. The nightingale I hear on a May night is not a prototype, a rough-cast early link in the Great Chain of Being that leads inexorably upwards to Bach or Keats, but a complete and finished creature, different from me in ways that I cannot even imagine, yet still able to move me. Its 'otherness' is precisely what touches me, more even than the common ecological threads between us. By 'singing itself' in such a pure and irreducibly musical way it seems to challenge and chasten any listeners singing *less* than themselves.

Listening to nightingales with a new respect over recent years, I have found those 'self-same songs' oddly reassuring. They provided consolation during the break-up of a relationship and a thread of continuity that helped keep us friends afterwards. (I was pleased to discover that nightingales have 'friendly' sub-songs, too – relaxed, unterritorial carollings in the tropical woods in winter.) They have continued to keep loneliness and anxiety at bay in strange places. But I have heard the ominous silence of sites that nightingales have abandoned, too, and know that the myths and metaphorical power cannot survive without the real bird.

This is the theme of what must be the most sympathetic and respectful of all nightingale stories. The bird in Hans Christian Andersen's tale lives in the woods surrounding the lavish palace of a Chinese emperor. He is summoned to court to sing, and enchants not just the Emperor but the whole population. But one day a parcel arrives for the Emperor containing an artificial nightingale, ornamented with jewels and driven by clockwork. The court, capricious as ever, is charmed, and the mechanical bird is set up for a duet with the real nightingale. It is a disastrous experiment. The mechanical bird keeps strict tempo and jars terribly with the free-flowing style of the real bird, which promptly flies back to the woods.

For a while the artificial nightingale is all the rage. It sings the same predictable, precisely measured song every time. The citizens learn to whistle its tune. The palace band perform concerts with it. Then, five years later, the Emperor falls fatally sick. The mechanical bird is worn out and past helping him. But, at the last moment, the real nightingale begins to sing outside the Emperor's window, and pulls him back to life. (Death flies out of the window, struck by 'a yearning for his garden'.) The Emperor implores the nightingale to stay with him, but the bird offers instead another kind of relationship:

> I can't make any home at the palace, but do you let me come here when I like. Then I will sit at evening time on the branch there by this window and sing to you, to make you happy, and thoughtful too. I will sing about the happy and about those who suffer. I will sing of the evil and the good that is about you and is hidden from you.

Softened though it is for a children's story, this is the same nightingale – wild, free-spirited, truly romantic – that sang for Keats and Coleridge, that held listeners spellbound in front of crackly 1920s radios, that I heard myself under a May full moon in Suffolk and that John Clare crouched close to, listening to an elegy for the old woodlands that were being flattened around him. It is the nightingale in which the real and metaphorical birds merge, and its song is a challenge to despair, a symbol of freedom, a hymn to individuality and difference, one way of celebrating what it feels like to be alive in this place at this moment. 'A year ago', Hardy wrote, these birds were only 'particles of grain,/And earth, and air, and rain'. Now, emphasised by their darkling setting, they are startling examples of the continually mysterious emergence of beauty from matter.

Notes and References

vii Lord Grey of Fallodon, *The Charm of Birds*, 1927

4 Alfred Tennyson, 'Aylmers Field'

7 Percy Bysshe Shelley, Semichorus from 'Prometheus Unbound', 1820

12 Matthew Arnold, 'Philomela'

13 Garth Christian, 'Listening to Nightingales', from *Down the Long Wind*, 1961

21–22 Stanley Cramp (ed.), *The Birds of the Western Palearctic*, Vol V., Oxford, 1988

23 Edward A. Armstrong, *A Study of Bird Song*, New York, 1973

24–25 Margaret Grainger (ed.), *The Natural History Prose Writings of John Clare*, Oxford, 1983

25–26 H.E. Bates, *Through the Woods*, 1936

29–30 Pliny, *Natural History*, Book X

30–31 Olina, *Uccelliera*, 1662.

33 Richard Jefferies, 'Nightingales'. First published in the *St James's Gazette*, April 1886. See also: W.B. Yarrell, *A History of British Birds*, 1872–4 'Nightingales who change their tune', *New Scientist*, 14 March 1992

34 Francis Willughby, *The Ornithology*, 1628

35 Peggy Munsterberg (ed.), *Bird Poetry*, 1980

38 Sally Festing, *Gertrude Jekyll*, London and New York, 1991

42 Edward A. Armstrong, 'The Evolution of Man's Appreciation of Birdsong', in R. A. Hinde (ed.), *Bird Vocalisations*, Cambridge, 1969

46–7 P. Stuttard and K. Williamson, 'Habitat requirements of the nightingale', *Bird Study* 18, 1971 Kevin Bayne and Andrew Henderson, 'Nightingales and coppice woodland', *RSPB Conservation Review*, 1988

R.J. Fuller, 'Distribution of breeding songbirds in Bradfield Woods, Suffolk in relation to vegetation and coppice management', *Bird Study*, 39, 1992

49 quoted in *A Watch of Nightingales*, ed. Geoffrey Keynes and Peter Davidson, The Stourton Press, 1981

51 A thirteenth-century biography of St Thibaut grouped nightingales with other kinds of perniciously seductive voices, and obviously felt their metaphorical meaning was well enough known to need no further explanation: 'We must abandon the field of the Sirens and those of the nightingale, who makes many insane, and in all ways we must become stronger so that we may near the kingdom of Jesus Christ.'

52–55 Wendy Pfeffer, *The Change of Philomel: The nightingale in medieval literature*, New York, 1985. See also: Beryl Rowlands, *Birds with Human Souls*, University of Tennessee Press, 1978

55–56 *The Lais of Marie de France*, translated and edited by Glyn S. Burgess, 1986

J.P. Clancy (ed.), *Medieval Welsh Lyrics*, 1965

56 Though affection for the bird wasn't universal in Britain. Mary Woodward's poem 'Nightingales' relates the story of a medieval hermit buried in St Albans Abbey who routed the nightingales from his wood 'because their song disturbed his prayer': 'Imagine the silent trees, the man alone there making his continuous lonely devotion to nothing./ And the brown birds' throats warm with joy and music gone for ever.'

60–61 Cecil Sharp, *English Folk Song from the Southern Appalachians*, 1966

65–68 Richard Holmes, *Coleridge: Early Visions*, 1989

H.W. Garrod, *Keats*, 1926

Robert Gittings, *John Keats*, 1968

Robert Gittings, *John Keats: The living year*, 1954

68 Keats wrote a little panegyric to his sister on 1 May
   containing images similar to those in the ode: 'Please
   heaven, a little claret-wine cool out of a cellar a mile
   deep . . . a strawberry bed to say your prayers to
   Flora in.'

69–70 Janet Spens, 'A study of Keats's "Ode to a
   Nightingale" ', *Review of English Studies*, Vol. III,
   1952

74 Kenneth Grahame, *The Wind in the Willows*, 1908

85–86 John Clare, 'The Nightingale's Nest' first
   published in *The Midsummer Cushion*, ed. Anne
   Tibble, 1978

87 Gilbert White, *The Natural History of Selborne*, 1789
   Kim Taplin, 'Possession', in *Second Nature*, ed.
   Richard Mabey, 1984

91–93 Margaret Grainger (ed.), *op.cit.*

91 Hugh Haughton, 'To look on nature with a poetic
   eye: John Clare's "The Nightingale's Nest" and
   romantic poetry', 1991 in press

94 John Berger, 'The White Bird' from *The White Bird*,
   1985

95 Steven Povey, 'The Birds of Selborne', *The Selborne
   Association Newsletter*, 32, 1991
   M.E.S. Rooney, 'A report on the status of bird
   species at Castor Hanglands National Nature
   Reserve, 1957–1985', Internal Nature Conservancy
   Council report

96 J.T.R. Sharrock, *The Atlas of Breeding Birds in Britain
   and Ireland*, British Trust for Ornithology, 1976

99 R. Chislett, *Yorkshire Birds*, 1952

99–102 Beatrice Harrison, *The Cello and the Nightingale*,
   ed. Patricia Cleveland-Peck, 1985

105 Messiaen's notes translated by the pianist Peter Hill

106 David Hindley, 'The music of birdsong', *The Wildlife
   Sound Journal*, Vol. 6 No. 4, Autumn 1990
   Joan Hall-Craggs, 'The aesthetic content of bird
   song', in R.A. Hinde (ed.), *Bird Vocalisations*,
   Cambridge, 1969
   Edward A. Armstrong, 1973 *op.cit.*

108 Charles Hartshorne, 'The relation of bird song to music', *Ibis*, 100, 1958
    David Raines Wallace, *Bulow Hammock*, Sierra Club, San Francisco, 1988. See also: Lewis Thomas, 'The music of *this* sphere' in *The Lives of a Cell*, New York, 1974
109 Cecil Sharp, 1966 *op.cit.*
    See Kit Wright's poem 'The sub-song' in *Short Afternoons*, 1989
110 Hans Christian Andersen, 'The Nightingale', trans. M.R. James, London and New York, 1972

Acknowledgements

My thanks to friends who have listened to nightingales with me, especially Roy Adams, Francesca Greenoak, Rachel Hamilton, Robin Hamilton, John Kilpatrick, Anne Mallinson and Peter Newmark.

To Nicola Bion and Alan Cudmore for locating (and lending) elusive books; the staff of the Bodleian library; Benny Green, for illuminating some of the history of 'A Nightingale Sang in Berkeley Square'; Sally Haines and her staff in the BBC's Sound Archives; Hugh Haughton, for allowing me to see the unpublished manuscript of his paper on Clare's 'The Nightingale's Nest'; Chris Mead, Robert Fuller and Philip Jackson at the British Trust for Ornithology; Bill Mitchell, whose advice was so helpful at a tangled point in the text; Jane Stemp, librarian at Lady Margaret Hall, Oxford; Richard Williamson; Kit Wright, for his poem, 'The sub-song'.

To Penny Hoare at Sinclair-Stevenson for her patience and editorial advice.

And to the friends with whom I had such exhilarating and illuminating discussions about nightingales: Ronnie Blythe for his continued encouragement and his insights into Keats's Ode; Jeff Cloves, who urged me (successfully I hope) to reveal more of my own feelings, and who read the finished text with an inspired eye; David Cobham, who took a wise and objective view of the text; David Hindley, for sharing the revelations of his musical analysis of bird song; Philip Oswald, for thoughts and material on the classical view of nightingales that would have made a whole book in themselves; and Richard Simon, who, as always, was throughout the course of the book a source of support and common sense.

Index